Competency-based Education
and Assessment

Competency-based Education and Assessment

The Excelsior Experience

Edited by

Tina Goodyear

Foreword by Pamela Tate
Introduction by John Ebersole

HUDSON
WHITMAN
EXCELSIOR COLLEGE PRESS

Published in the United States by
Hudson Whitman/ Excelsior College Press
7 Columbia Circle, Albany, NY 12203
www.hudsonwhitman.com

Printed in the United States of America
Book design by Sue Morreale
Cover design by Phil Pascuzzo

Library of Congress
Cataloging-in-publication data

LCCN 2016943179

ISBN: 978-1-944079-03-1

Contents

Foreword

Pamela Tate

President and CEO, CAEL

Since the Council for Adult and Experiential Learning (CAEL) has been working in the field of prior learning assessment (PLA) and competency-based education (CBE) for over forty years, we have been involved in PLA and CBE at every stage of their development in higher education. What is interesting about the current resurgence of CBE—estimates from a study in 2015 show that over 600 institutions were implementing CBE programs in various stages—is that it is being promoted primarily as a degree completion accelerator and a cost-saver in many states, and as a better way to prepare students for the workforce. In contrast, CBE in its early years—the years during which Excelsior began its competency-based nursing program—was primarily about increasing access for the underserved adult learner and ensuring that their learning would be recognized and counted. The idea that what a person knows and can do is more important than where or how the person learned it, an idea that has inspired both CAEL and Excelsior over the past four decades, is central to both CBE and PLA; this book reinforces my view that Excelsior's approach to CBE—while responsive to employer needs and to cost savings concerns—still embodies the access goal we have worked so hard to reach. Yes, CBE can accelerate a student's progress to a degree;

yes, it can save the student money and time—as can PLA; and yes, CBE is likely to enable graduates to be more prepared employees—but we cannot lose the core principle that CBE can open doors for those adults who might otherwise not be able to afford and finish higher education.

As we have carried out an increasing amount of research, training, and consulting with institutions and accreditors in CBE and PLA over the past several years, I have observed several trends: 1) Institutions are confused about what is meant by CBE and what their accreditor's response might be to their CBE plans; 2) Institutions are wary of the Department of Education's mixed messages on CBE, PLA, and other innovations related to non-traditional providers of postsecondary education; 3)Institutions are being pursued by a range of technology vendors with varying levels of expertise and cost proposals, and do not know to what extent these new technologies are useful; 4) Institutions are not doing enough to train their faculty and staff on these approaches so that they can be implemented with both rigor and enthusiasm; and 5) Institutions rarely have the assessment expertise and knowledge to undertake a true CBE approach at the outset—this capability must be built and nurtured over time.

In this complicated climate, Excelsior's book provides not only a good theoretical approach to defining and assessing competencies, but also includes practical, on-the-ground approaches that Excelsior has developed over decades, which can guide many other institutions embarking on this CBE path. The chapters on the two highlighted programs—Excelsior's groundbreaking CBE-based nursing program, built over forty years ago, and its recently-developed CBE business degree—are detailed, straightforward descriptions of program assumptions, design and challenges—all of which can help other institutions navigate CBE waters more easily. I believe that Excelsior can serve as a community of practice leader in this field and that this book is an important contribution to that thought leadership role.

What struck me as I read the book is the importance Excelsior places on having an assessment approach that is built upon psychometric expertise and assessment of performance, while at the same time, paying close attention to providing students with service and support. In addition, the book describes in some detail how the college has tried to deal with the challenges of satisfying licensing bodies, responding to industry standards, and meeting the skills needs of employers without sacrificing the broader learning goals of an undergraduate degree. The fact that Excelsior is able to draw upon a rich and successful history of CBE in nursing—one that is grounded in valid and reliable assessment—can give others who are newer to the field confidence in how to proceed as well as tactical strategies for embedding CBE approaches in the entire undergraduate experience.

As in any emerging field, there are risks and difficult questions, including: Will the role of faculty be diminished or enhanced? Will institutions attempt to innovate but find that the Department of Education's ambiguity on CBE is creating too much of a barrier to proceed? Can institutions implement CBE initiatives without investing too much up-front in technology solutions? Will students have difficulty transferring if they have been in a CBE program and are moving to another institution without this option? If institutions learn from CBE leaders like Excelsior, I believe they can avoid some of the pitfalls and sustain their CBE efforts—so I am delighted this book is being published especially at this time. CAEL's staff and consultants will certainly be using it as a resource in our next stage of work with colleges and universities.

Introduction

John Ebersole
President of Excelsior College

When the idea of creating a practitioner's guide to CBE was first proposed, we immediately recognized the time had finally arrived for Excelsior to contribute its expertise. As we monitored the developing national discourse and worked to create a focus for the guide, several observations about CBE emerged: There are and will continue to be multiple and diverging definitions of competency-based education; the number of and types of institutions engaged in the development and implementation of CBE programs is expanding and is not going to disappear any time soon; and, most importantly, the critical role of assessment—that is, how to measure the *application* of knowledge, skills and abilities, not merely its possession—the true foundation of a sound CBE program, was missing from the national conversation. While most agree that a student's competency must be assessed, there is little information or collective experience about *how* to create and deliver a psychometrically sound assessment of competency. This is where we saw Excelsior's expertise—four decades of rigorously defining and applying assessment—to be of most use.

A clearer understanding of assessment begins with a brief illustration of Excelsior's foundational mission, a directive to develop alternative pathways to degree completion. In 1971, after its founding by the Regents of the State of New York, the college (which carried the "Regents" name until 2001), with funding and expertise from the Kellogg Foundation, launched a process for earning an associate degree which then, as now, provides the basic education requirement for becoming an RN, a Registered Nurse.

Regents' model recognized learning gained from experience, as it augmented knowledge required for degree completion. Controversially, clinical skills were not taught as part of our nursing program, and clinical preceptorships were not required (a major bottleneck for traditional programs today). Instead, admission was limited to licensed health care workers with multiple years of experience. This included, over time, a large percentage of LPN/LVNs (80%), senior military corpsmen, paramedics, and licensed health care specialties such as respiratory therapists.

While it was expected that these students would come with considerable clinical experience, we kept with President Reagan's philosophy: "trust, but verify." Together, Regents and Kellogg Foundation designed the associate in nursing program to provide content knowledge in a number of areas, and to *assess* (verify) clinical competence. This verification was done through a multi-day, hands-on assessment, conducted under the trained eyes of graduate prepared nurse educators, in a real hospital, with real patients. This continues to be the case.

Decades later, associate degree nursing applicants are still screened for length and type of experience. Those admitted have the option of studying independently or through an online program. Both are now approved for Title IV financial aid. In either case, eight areas of content are assessed and must be passed in order to move to the capstone Clinical Performance Nursing Exam (CPNE). The clinical skills expected of an RN are, as they have always been, verified, measured, assessed, and held as a condition of graduation.

To date, tens of thousands of aspiring RNs have successfully completed the associate degree program, with 18,000 currently enrolled. The student body is large, national, and diverse (90% reside in states other than New York) and are able to sit for, or transfer, their licensure into every state except, as of 2016, California.

Certainly, competency-based assessment can be considerably more difficult for students; as such, this model has been and is still subjected to frequent review and validation from both a probability and content perspective. While the model has its detractors, it has never been found deficient in either reliability or validity. Several of the more interesting legal challenges we faced and surmounted are addressed at length in the Appendix. We hope educators considering a licensure environment will see these examples as useful cautions.

For those of us who educate adult, posttraditional, or other students outside of the 18-22-year-old sector, CBE is technically not new. It is true, though, that the CBE movement has gained visibility and momentum over the past few years. Due to three factors, the need for quality assessment has snowballed. The first is the increasing irrelevance of the credit hour as a metric. As Amy Laitinen noted in her eye-opening 2012 critique, *Cracking the Credit Hour*, the credit hour may be needed for financial aid administration, but it is little more than a surrogate time in a seat. It doesn't measure outcomes of any type and is not suited to the many forms of alternative instructional delivery that exist today. In contrast, CBE, if it involves rigorous assessment methods, provides some assurance of both learning and an ability to apply it.

The second has come from the Obama Administration and its attempts to see more working adults complete their degrees, thus contributing to our country's economic competitiveness. By recognizing the legitimacy of knowledge gained from experiences outside of a traditional classroom, post traditional students are incentivized through the CBE process by reducing both the cost and the time needed to achieve a degree. A win-win.

The third, and arguably the most important reason for the growth of CBE, is the increasing dissatisfaction of employers with the typical college graduate. The lengthening period between graduation and employment that many students experience can be attributed partially to the practice of employers seeking a more capable alternative before settling on a recent graduate. If we can demonstrate to ourselves and to employers that it is producing "competent" entrants to the workforce, it is not just the new hire, their alma mater, and the employer who win. We all do.

In the desire to embrace this important form of credentialing, there are reasons for excitement, optimism, and concern. Dr. Paul LeBlanc, president of Southern New Hampshire University, in his testimony before Congress (2015) expressed a need to proceed slowly. While some heard his testimony as a call to limit experimentation and institutional participation, our view is that he is merely emphasizing the great need to get CBE right. Thus, we shall all continue our efforts, but at a pace that allows for conversations, sharing of experiences, lessons learned, and refinements.

In addition to moving too fast, and producing programs under a "let a thousand flowers bloom" strategy, there are concerns about best practices, definitions, and coordination. Where, for instance, can an institution turn for help in creating programs and rigorous assessments that address both the criticism and needs expressed?

This guide provides essential preliminary direction with an emphasis on the principles of assessment, applying the language of assessment, using assessment principles in determining competency, and finally illustrating principles in action. We do not see this work addressing all that is needed, but we believe that through continued sharing of lessons learned, we can build a body of knowledge equal to the need.

In the chapters that follow, Dr. Patrick Jones, Excelsior's Vice Provost and former head of Excelsior's Center for Educational Measurement (CEM), with assistance from Dr. Mika Hoffman, Executive Director of Test Development Services within the Center for Educational Measurement, discuss the complexities and need for an assessment process that reliably and accurately determines both knowledge levels and the ability to apply that knowledge in a way that demonstrates true competence. We have all met individuals who have dazzled us with their understanding of a subject or discipline but were ineffective in their attempts to act on, or apply, what they knew. This, as Dr. Jones points out, is what we hope to avoid.

Dr. Mary Lee Pollard and Dr. Karl Lawrence share their perspectives regarding essential ingredients for a successful competency-based program. Dr. Pollard oversees the decades-old and very successful Associates Degree in Nursing program. She and her staff are focused on the needs of thousands of aspiring RN's, who if not for the CBE format, might never achieve the degree, license, salary, and commensurate professional opportunities that come with licensure.

Dr. Lawrence, as dean of the School of Business and Technology, and his executive director of accreditation, Dr. Scott Dolan, are currently leading the college's efforts to create a new competency-based path to an undergraduate degree in business. As you will read, this has been especially challenging as the team had to build consensus around needed competencies, how they are to be assessed, and by whom. While many of the school's faculty are drawn from the business community, there is also a need to include prospective employers in the process.

With our long history comes hard-earned wisdom and many lessons learned. This guide has been created to share those lessons for the benefit of other educators and institutions, our students (who need alternate and sound pathways to degree completion), and ultimately, our nation, as it regains its place in a competitive global environment.

Chapter 1

Assessment

What We've Learned and Why It Matters

John Ebersole

President of Excelsior College

Tina Goodyear

Executive Director for Assessment of Post-Traditional Instruction, Training, and Learning

Assessment is one of most important aspects of any competency-based program. It is also one of the more difficult. In essence, assessment provides a type of certification or guarantee that the graduates receiving the degree in this manner have been found competent, not only in terms of their knowledge in a particular discipline, but that they also have the ability to apply that knowledge in an employment setting or for further study at a higher level. Thus, there are a number of questions Excelsior should be able to answer if asked about what many see as a new pathway to a degree, competency-based education. Those kinds of questions may include, "What are the core competencies that have been assessed?," "Who does the assessing?," and most importantly, "How do you know the graduate is competent, especially in the performance assessment?"

It is from these critical questions, and Excelsior's foundation in assessment, that we offer thee significant lessons learned when considering assessment in CBE. These lessons frame this guidebook and are each addressed in more detail in the chapters that follow.

Lesson 1: Assessment, regardless of format or method, must adhere to sound psychometric principles.

Chapter two will make a strong argument that a well thought out assessment process supports the actions and knowledge to be evaluated, as well as clarifies who will be performing such an assessment. Perhaps, more importantly in the CBE context, the most critical question answered by a sound assessment is how we know the graduate is competent. More specifically, how do we know that our process is reliable, valid, and capable of being defended as statistically accurate? These can be complicated questions requiring skill in the field of assessment to answer. Although Excelsior is fortunate to have this specialized knowledge through its Center for Educational Measurement, and adheres to standards put forth by well-regarded evaluation associations, the college still relies on further confirmation from third-party evaluators, like the American Council on Education (ACE), to validate its process and outcomes. As a result, our oldest CBE degree program in nursing and its assessment procedure (the CPNE, Clinical Professional Nursing Examination), has become widely recognized as meeting the national standards of care and state licensing mandates.

Lesson 2: Assessment in CBE must include a strong performance component.

Success in meeting such rigorous requirements hinges on more than simply assessing student knowledge. In CBE, it is critical to assess students' ability to apply knowledge and to assess their performance in terms of meeting competency in the field. As evidenced in the development of Excelsior's CPNE (See Chapter 3), one important step in the CBE process is to create a common language between performance expectations in industry and those of higher education through the development of clear competencies that link to the priorities of both.

Without that crosswalk, performance assessment will not meet validity and reliability requirements. If a CBE-degreed graduate is found to be *not* able to perform functions considered key to a task or job, the negative consequences can be expected to be severe. They will be particularly severe if the inability repeats multiple times, in multiple graduates. As educators, if we do not address the psychometric accuracy of those performance assessments, we will have expended much effort on a process that fails to achieve the desired outcome, and will soon lose all credibility.

Lesson 3: Assessment in CBE must align with industry standards and employers' needs.

Recent interest in CBE may have sprung from the fact that the credibility of higher education has already been questioned by the employment community. There is a wide disparity in the perception of employers and institutions regarding graduates' preparedness for the workforce. This disparity, however, sets the stage for CBE to encourage synergy between the two sectors.

Consider that less than three in ten employers think that college graduates are well prepared for the workplace, specifically in the areas of critical thinking, written and oral communication, and the application of knowledge and skills in real-world settings. Yet over half of academic provosts surveyed report their institutions "very effective" at preparing students for work, with another 40% reporting their institutions as "somewhat effective" (Jaschik, 2014).

Employers cannot wait for the discrepancy in perception to fix itself. To meet demand for qualified workers, companies often create their own skills-based competency training for new graduates. Some estimates indicate that employers are spending, collectively, nearly $590 billion a year on employee learning through a combination of structured and informal learning; yet, our nation is still experiencing a significant skills gap in high demand areas (Carnevale, 2015).

One important way for institutions to become more active and innovative partners with employers entails aligning outcomes (or competencies) with the needs of those employers, as Excelsior College did in creating its CBE capstone in the School of Business and Technology (see Chapter 4). This model is premised on the fact that, as both educators and employers agree, knowledge acquisition will do little to improve overall employee and organizational productivity if that knowledge is not readily applicable in the context of the work environment.

These changes are helping to reduce the divide between vocational and liberal education, and CBE—with its focus on assessing the application of skills—has the potential to provide that closure. To be sure, that closure will only be possible if the assessment process proves to be a valid and reliable indicator of results that align with employer expectations and are evidenced by employee performance after hire.

Also of great concern as CBE moves forward is the acceptance of such degrees at the graduate level. In much the same way that CBE must prove its rigor and relevance to industry, graduate programs will need to see continual evidence that our undergraduates are prepared for higher learning. Sound assessment in the CBE environment can help provide assurance that alternative forms of learning meet requirements of the academy as well.

References

Carnevale, A., Stohl, J., & Gulish, A. (2015). *College is Just the Beginning.* Georgetown University, Center on Education and the Workforce, McCourt School of Public Policy. Retrieved from https://cew.georgetown. edu/wp-content/uploads/2015/02/Trillion-Dollar-Training-System-.pdf

Jaschik, S. (2014, January 23). Pressure on the provosts: 2014 survey of chief academic officers. *Inside Higher Ed.* Retrieved from https:// www.insidehighered.com/news/survey/pressure-provosts-2014-survey-chief-academic-officers

Chapter 2

Principles of Assessment
A Primer

Mika Hoffman

Executive Director of Test Development Services

Patrick Jones

Vice Provost and Former Dean of Assessment

Introduction

Although there may be uncertainty in higher education surrounding the definition and viability of CBE, one thing is clear: assessment is critical.

There are two uses of the term "assessment" that need to be disambiguated from the start: the first, which we will address in this chapter, is used to make evaluations of or decisions about **individuals**. The second, also known as outcomes assessment or institutional effectiveness, is used to make evaluations of or decisions about **programs**, and is beyond the scope of this chapter.

In order to make claims about what students know and can do, schools need a clear basis for judgment. Perhaps the most significant takeaway from Excelsior's experience, then, is the importance of using sound assessment strategies to promote best practices in CBE. Excelsior began to establish its expertise in direct assessment in the early 1970s, and today the college's Center for Educational Measurement offers over sixty UExcel credit-bearing proficiency exams; our Associate Degree in Nursing (ADN) program was founded as an assessment-based program, and includes a clinical performance assessment, as well as proficiency examinations. Before diving into the details of these competency-based exams, it is important to discuss the principles and strategies that guide the development, scoring, and revision of assessments. The incorporation of these principles and strategies into the context of a competency environment will be illustrated in the chapters that follow.

Assessment in a CBE Environment

What is assessment? It is more than creating a test that arbitrarily gives anyone who scores more than 90% a grade of "A." It is part of an educational process that includes

- establishing clear, measurable outcomes of student learning,

- ensuring that students have sufficient opportunities to achieve those outcomes,

- systematically gathering, analyzing, and interpreting evidence to determine how well student learning matches expectations, and

- using the resulting information to understand and improve student learning (Suskie, 2009, p. 23).

The second bullet is not part of assessment development itself (although it is important for the quality of the educational program!), but the other three provide a good perspective on the goals of assessment.

All assessments have the same general purpose: to generate information that will be used to make decisions. In educational assessment, decisions can range from what to focus on in the next lesson to whether a student can be admitted to or graduate from a program. The common thread is that they generate information about the achievement levels of students relative to established guidelines and expectations. In traditional programs, expectations might include "grading on a curve," in which scores reflect where an examinee ranks in a group, for example in cases in which instructors must limit the number of "A" grades to a certain percentage of the class. Such scoring rules, known as norm-referenced assessment, are useful if you want to rank people. But they are not useful if you want to know whether a student has attained a competency.

In a competency-based education (CBE) program, the guidelines and expectations must be clearly defined based on competency definitions, curriculum requirements, and institutional standards. **CBE requires criterion-referenced assessment**: the score is tied to standards for the competency, and what one student does has no effect on another student's score.

An important objective in a competency environment is to provide students, faculty and administrators with accurate, precise, and consistent information that can be used to inform teaching and learning activities in real time or to make decisions about student attainment of competencies. These requirements can place a heavy burden on assessment developers and users to assure that assessment methods are effective. To put the burden in context, consider some common challenges in creating a sound CBE assessment.

- It is often difficult for professionals in a given occupation to reach consensus on the definition of professionalism or required competencies within their field, yet such agreement is critical for the creation of measurable competency statements (Epstein, 2007).

- It is important to select assessment content that clearly aligns with the target knowledge, skills, abilities, and competencies, but the assessment results also need to provide evidence that students have mastered the knowledge, skills, abilities, and competencies, rather than just memorized facts or process steps. Thus, the content cannot be just the same material students have already practiced (Good, 2011, p. 3–4).

- It is difficult to find an assessment format that is both appropriate for measuring the student learning outcomes (knowledge, skills, abilities, and competencies) and that will also produce consistent results, while at the same time keeping costs and staff time requirements at a reasonable level.

- It can be challenging to meet the need for personalized student learning feedback while simultaneously maintaining a standard and consistent approach to assessment.

A deeper look at the fundamental principles of assessment, such as validity and reliability, and their application to the CBE environment can help educators and test developers as they strive to overcome these challenges.

Validity and Reliability

Given the importance of decisions concerning student progress and the awarding of degrees and credentials, how can schools evaluate the quality of the assessments that form the basis for those decisions? Assessment quality is usually described in terms of **validity** (relating to accuracy) and **reliability** (relating to consistency or precision). The popular media often misuse the terms validity and reliability by discussing an assessment *tool* as valid and/or reliable; in fact, it is the *inferences* based on the results of the assessment, not the assessment tool itself, that should be evaluated in terms of validity and reliability.

The results of a given assessment can be used in valid or invalid ways. For example, scores on a nursing quiz on dosage calculations may be validly used to determine if a student understands how to do dosage calculations, but not to make decisions about whether the student can perform injections. With respect to reliability, a market research project assignment might yield very different grades depending on how much time students are given to complete it, so two students of equal ability might get different grades if one was given one week to complete it and another was given four weeks; using the grade from that project to determine ability to use market research techniques would not yield consistent predictions. So specifying the intended inference to be made is critical.

Why are the concepts of validity and reliability of such critical importance in a CBE assessment environment? They are foundational for all assessments, of course, but there are three reasons why they are particularly important for CBE. First, the claims made by CBE programs tend to be strong and specific: a student has or has not attained a defined competency. In traditional programs, passing a course usually means there's a reasonable expectation that the student has grasped most of the important concepts, but not necessarily that the student has mastered each of a specific list of outcomes. Second, in CBE programs there is often more weight given to formal assessments, since elements such as attendance, class participation, or homework completion are often not considered. In traditional programs, many more individual assessments (formal and informal) typically make up the final grade, so there is less need for each one to provide a lot of useful information. A third consideration is external: because CBE programs tend to be new, they are judged in comparison to traditional programs; and the burden is heavier on CBE programs than on traditional programs to show that students come out learning what they should.

So what can we do to make sure CBE assessment results are used in a valid way? It should be apparent that the choice of assessment content and format, the method of administering the assessment, how it is scored, and other factors will contribute to the overall usefulness of the results to make decisions, and some of these issues are discussed below. But it is important to remember that even a well-constructed and reliably scored assessment may not produce results that can be validly used for a particular purpose, especially if the assessment was originally designed for different purposes. Documenting all aspects of assessment development is crucial in order to provide the information that academic program managers, instructors, students, employers, and others will need to determine whether their decisions are resting on a solid foundation.

Validity

Validity is the most important concept in assessment. It is complex, and views about how to understand its complexities have changed over time. In 2016, the approach is to focus on validation as an argument: the responsibility of assessment developers is to produce *evidence* for the use of the assessment results to make the intended decisions. There are five types of validity evidence: 1—relating to content, 2—response processes, 3—internal structure, 4—external variables, and 5—consequences (American Educational Research Association, American Psychological Association, & National Council on Measurement in Education, 2014; Downing, 2003; McClarty & Gaertner, 2015). Ideally, each use of any assessment should provide evidence of all five types, although the particular evidence will vary widely depending on the nature of the assessment.

The multiple types of validity evidence may seem daunting. But to have a credible program, it is crucial to understand what assessment results mean *and* to be confident in the decisions made based on those results (McClarty & Gaertner, 2015). There are a few basic steps that can have a big impact. Before exploring these steps, following is a brief look at each type of validity evidence.

Evidence from Content, Response Processes, and Internal Structure

These types of evidence reflect how the assessment content is developed: what is covered, the types of tasks and formats used, and how the tasks or items work together. Content evidence is usually what assessment brings to mind first: is the content of the assessment aligned to the competency statement or learning outcome? Problems arise if the competency encompasses broad areas of knowledge and the assessment entails an essay focusing on one area only. Closely linked to content evidence is evidence about response processes: what tasks do the students need to perform to demonstrate competency? An accounting exam that requires students to read lengthy scenarios may produce more information about reading ability than about application of accounting principles. Sometimes programs may be tempted to repurpose traditional final exams as competency assessments, but in many cases final exams may focus on knowledge of facts, whereas the competency may require synthesis or application. Internal structure evidence tends to focus on the measurement quality of the components: is scoring consistent? Are the tasks actually distinguishing between those who have mastered the competency and those who have not?

Questions to Consider about Content, Response Processes, and Internal Structure

(1) What are the precise competencies and knowledge domains to be assessed and who determines them?
(2) Are all the domains represented on the assessment in some way? If not, what would show that mastery of domains covered by the assessment is evidence for mastery of those not covered?
(3) Are the tasks aligned to the competencies, without interference from other factors such as reading or writing ability (in cases where reading and writing are not the competency in question)?
(4) Are all students equally familiar or unfamiliar with the content (for example, have they all seen the essay prompt in advance, or is it a surprise to all of them what task they will need to perform)?
(5) Is it clear to students what they need to do?
(6) Do the people rating performance rate consistently and according to the same criteria?

Evidence from External Variables and Consequences

External variables and consequences should be considered when using performance on the assessment to make a decision about mastery. Do the results of the assessment tend to correlate with expectations among faculty and industry about what competent individuals should know and be able to do—that is, do people passing the assessment enter the workforce actually able to use the competency? The most important piece to consider in this regard, and a frequently overlooked piece, is the method of determining what the passing score is. Suppose an assessment of presentation skills involves having students prepare ten PowerPoint slides on a particular subject and then present them orally, with faculty rating the presentations according to several criteria (speed of delivery, tone of voice, body language, flow, etc.). Does a student who fails on one criterion but passes the rest ultimately pass or fail the assessment? Or suppose students take a multiple-choice test to assess their knowledge of the airborne transmission of disease. What score would indicate that they have mastered the content?

Questions to Consider about External Variables and Consequences

(1) Are students who pass the assessment able to use the assessed skill in practice?

(2) What methods were used to determine the passing score? Were these methods aligned with the definition of the level of proficiency required for mastery? Do they take into account what happens if there are different versions of the assessment that may involve harder or easier tasks?

(3) What happens to students who fail—do they take the same assessment later, or a different version of it?

What You Can Do

Clearly, valid assessment score use requires good alignment between the tasks and the competency, and between how the tasks are scored and the performance level required. How can this alignment be ensured? As a starting point, three things must be in place: a **plan**, a **review process**, and **alignment** of scores to standards (See Figure 1 below). Bearing in mind that validation is an argument for a connection between assessment results and a decision, a **plan** facilitates advanced thinking about how to provide evidence for that connection.

A **review process** is crucial for maximizing item or task quality. Problems with item and task quality are considered by some assessment

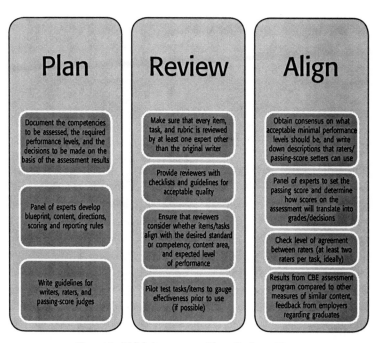

Plan

Document the competencies to be assessed, the required performance levels, and the decisions to be made on the basis of the assessment results

Panel of experts develop blueprint, content, directions, scoring and reporting rules

Write guidelines for writers, raters, and passing-score judges

Review

Make sure that every item, task, and rubric is reviewed by at least one expert other than the original writer

Provide reviewers with checklists and guidelines for acceptable quality

Ensure that reviewers consider whether items/tasks align with the desired standard or competency, content area, and expected level of performance

Pilot test tasks/items to gauge effectiveness prior to use (if possible)

Align

Obtain consensus on what acceptable minimal performance levels should be, and write down descriptions that raters/passing-score setters can use

Panel of experts to set the passing score and determine how scores on the assessment will translate into grades/decisions

Check level of agreement between raters (at least two raters per task, ideally)

Results from CBE assessment program compared to other measures of similar content, feedback from employers regarding graduates

Figure 1. Valid Assessment: Plan, Review, Align

professionals to be the most serious threat to validity. Most educators understand that it's important to have well-written items in order test precisely what is intended, or tasks that have clear instructions so that students know what they need to do. But actually achieving that takes more than just one expert writing a test or task instructions. Critical eyes are required to notice unclear or ambiguous language in the items, instructions, or rubrics, and to make sure that the components of the assessment cover the right tasks.

Just as important, **aligning** scores to standards is crucial for that validity argument. If an assessment consists of nicely written items but it's been arbitrarily decided that 70% is a passing score because that's usually a C, then the validity argument falls apart. The passing score should separate those students who have the competency from those who do not. Without careful consideration, there is no basis for thinking that any arbitrary number will make that separation.

Further discussion of some of the details of the Plan-Review-Align components follows, but first the basic concepts behind reliability must be addressed.

Reliability

Reliability refers to the stability and consistency of educational assessment results: people with the same levels of knowledge, skills, and ability should achieve the same results. Reliability is closely tied to validity, particularly with evidence related to internal structure. If assessment scores vary widely depending on whether students took the test at home or in the university testing center, for example, the stability and consistency of results would be challenged. Likewise, a performance work task scored by human raters that produces competence classifications that differ significantly by age group would suggest bias and inconsistent results. Low reliability typically points to problems involving a muddying of the assessment waters by factors other than what is actually being assessed.

It is helpful to think of reliability in the context of measurement error: when reliability is low, a mistake has been made somewhere in the assessment process. There are three main sources of error: 1) errors in the assessment design, 2) errors made during the assessment administration, and 3) errors made while scoring the assessment. Following is an examination of each source of error, and steps that can be taken to minimize each one.

**Questions to Consider about
Error due to Assessment Design**

(1) If any specific materials are needed to prepare, do all students have equal access to them?

(2) Do assessment tasks rely on assumptions about student background (for example, are the tasks contextualized in ways that are likely to be more accessible to one gender or cultural, educational, or employment background)?

(3) Are students supposed to know ahead of time what the specific assessment tasks are (for example, that they will have to perform CPR on a pediatric dummy, or that they will have to draw the locations of all the pulse points), or are the tasks supposed to be unknown?

Steps to minimize error due to assessment design include:

- Analyzing outcome patterns for students assessed at different times within a testing period or at different locations.

- Analyzing response patterns for individual assessment tasks. Students who do well on the assessment as a whole should be more likely than others to do any given particular task correctly. Also, on any given task students from one particular background, culture, age, or gender should not be performing differently from other students (unless their background is related to what is being assessed: for example, students who came to the program straight from high school might well do worse on a task for a human resources management assessment than students who came to the program after several years running a startup).

- Documenting any specific learning resources that are required, and ensuring that all students have equal access to them (in some cases it may be possible to document whether all students actually did access them). Learning resources should include a clear description of the assessment, sample questions and problems, an explanation of the consequences of student performance on each assessment, information on how the assessments are scored and the meaning of these scores, and a description of any strategies that will lead to optimal assessment performance.

- Documenting a plan to maintain the security and integrity of assessments. If students are not supposed to know the assessment content beforehand, steps should be taken to ensure there's no opportunity to see it.

- Ensuring that either (1) all students perform the same tasks (if the specific tasks are supposed to be public knowledge), or (2) there are multiple **equivalent** versions of the assessment, so that students are less likely to know ahead of time what questions will be asked.

- Ensuring the equivalence of different forms of the assessment. Use review by subject matter experts and analysis of assessment results at the form and question/problem level.

Questions to Consider about Scoring Error

(1) Are assessment data gathered accurately from all students (for example, are their responses handwritten, subject to error in deciphering them, or are they entered in a consistent way in a computer)?
(2) Are scoring and reporting rules consistently applied to results from all uses of the assessment?
(3) What are the qualifications of human raters and what steps are used to train and monitor human raters?

Steps to minimize scoring error include:

- Documenting quality control procedures during data collection, analysis, scoring, and reporting.

- Using machine- or computer-scored measures along with other quality controls.

- Documenting the qualifications, training, and experience of human raters along with a description of the steps used to monitor and intervene as needed.

- For human-rated tasks, using a rating rubric that all raters have been trained on, and ensuring that raters are not introducing criteria outside the rubric (for example, if an essay is to be used to test critical thinking, raters should not take points off for spelling).

- Ensuring that student names and other identifying information are not shared with human raters.

- Using more than one rater for any human-rated task.

- Reporting measures of inter-rater agreement and providing additional training to improve score consistency.

Questions to Consider about Administration Error

(1) Are the instructions to students clear?

(2) Do students understand the criteria that will be used to rate their performance?

(3) For assessments given in person, do those interacting with students stick to a consistent script, so that all students are given the same information?

(4) Are the conditions under which the assessment is given as similar as possible for all students (for example, type of room, presence of proctors, equivalent equipment)?

Steps to minimize administration error include:

- Documenting requirements for assessment locations (size of room, ventilation, heat, light, equipment).

- Documenting what proctors or exam administrators should say, so that all students have the same information about time limits, breaks, use of calculators or scratch paper, and other administration details.

- Documenting a process for reporting any administration problems so that patterns can be detected.

Some of the steps to reduce different types of error fit into the Plan-Review-Align process outlined in the section on validity. That is because, as mentioned earlier, reliability and validity are closely linked. Clearly, the Plan stage of documenting the assessment purpose, content, and rating and scoring principles is crucial to good measurement. By documenting plans ahead of time, inconsistencies or problems can be handled before they arise. The main test-planning document is sometimes referred to as a test specification, test plan, or blueprint. See the American Educational Research Association, American Psychological Association, and National

Council on Measurement in Education (2014) for helpful information about developing these documents.

CBE Assessment Development Guidelines

Following is a discussion of how the concepts of validity and reliability play out in three major areas: the content balance of the assessment, the format of the assessment tasks, and the performance level requirements. An important step in establishing the link between assessment performance and decisions resulting from that performance entails ensuring that assessment content and format are aligned with the competencies to be assessed, and that required performance levels are clearly thought through and documented. It is important to gather adequate input from qualified subject-matter experts and other stakeholder groups (e.g., industry, alumni, policy-makers) to inform decisions about how the competencies will be reflected in content, format, and scoring decisions.

Determining Specific Content and Format

(1) Define the breadth and depth of the target curriculum and learning resources.

(2) Create clear and concise statements reflecting the target knowledge, skills, abilities, and competencies, and delineations of the cognitive and psychomotor characteristics associated with competent performance.

(3) Document what type of evidence will be needed to determine whether a student has attained mastery of a given competency.

(4) Describe the assessment format models selected for target knowledge, skills, abilities, and competencies.

(5) Specify how much importance or weight will be placed on individual assessment activities.

In most educational assessment situations, a consensus process is employed to reach decisions on these matters. Most have done considerable work defining competencies and getting input from various stakeholders. The crucial point for assessment is that the statements must be **evidence-focused**. A clear statement of the competency only goes so far. How will the attainment of mastery of the competency be judged? Some measurements are more direct than others. For example, competency in oral presentation can usually be assessed by having a student give a presentation, but what factors about that presentation will be used to judge whether or not the competency has been mastered? And what would provide good evidence for the mastery of the principles of microbiology?

Assessment format is the way in which assessment tasks are presented, such as written responses, oral presentations, or multiple-choice questions. Decisions relating to assessment format play an important role in promoting the link between assessment results and the construct being measured. For example, it would not be appropriate to assess skills and competencies in areas such as oral communication, written expression, and psychomotor skills using an assessment featuring only multiple-choice questions; this format would not provide information reflective of student performance in these areas.

On the other hand, for an assessment that measures a grasp of a broad set of principles, using a format such as multiple choice, which can sample a great deal of content quickly, may be a good choice. In general, formats that allow for more creative student responses, such as essays and oral presentations, tend to be less stable, more prone to bias, and harder to rate appropriately than formats that constrain responses more closely, such as calculations or multiple-choice questions. And formats that constrain responses closely tend to be less forgiving of poor question-writing than formats that allow for more creative responses. Formats should be chosen with consideration not only for their positive characteristics but also their negative ones.

Guidelines for Assessment Format

(1) The assessment format must be appropriate for the content and target knowledge, skills, abilities, and competencies that comprise the curriculum.

(2) Formats should be selected based on their demonstrated ability to produce student responses that provide evidence leading to accurate, stable, and consistent inferences about a student's competency status.

(3) If more than one assessment method will satisfy all measurement quality and assessment specifications requirements, preference should be given to the method that is most efficient and cost effective.

(4) A sufficient number of assessment questions should be administered to allow students to demonstrate the appropriate levels of knowledge, skills, abilities, and competencies that represent the curriculum and learning resources. (The term "question" is intended to include all potential assessment formats, and the "appropriate level of student performance" is determined based on the goals and objectives of the assessment program.)

Determination and documentation of performance levels is a critical piece of assessment that is often overlooked. Many practitioners have a good sense for what constitutes acceptable performance, but sometimes different raters may disagree; so it is important to document and train raters on what acceptable performance looks like. For assessments that contain multiple tasks or questions, it is important to **define what acceptable performance is** on the assessment as a whole. Do students need to perform acceptably on each and every task? If not, what level of performance is acceptable? Two common approaches are the **compensatory** approach and the **non-compensatory** approach, as described below.

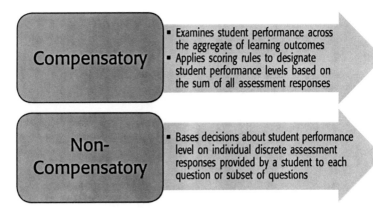

Figure 2. Common Scoring Approaches

The choice of approach will greatly impact the resources required to develop, administer, and score the summative assessment. Because non-compensatory scoring approaches rely on a high degree of accuracy and stability at each discrete assessment question level, this approach requires that a larger pool of assessment questions be developed, administered, and scored. There is a middle ground, in which subsets of tasks can be scored in a compensatory fashion, but each subset must be passed in order to attest that the student has attained the competency.

There are many methods for determining a passing score under the compensatory approach. For setting standards in high-stakes assessments, it is typical to convene an expert panel, in which panelists rate each task against a description of minimal acceptable performance and those decisions are aggregated in some way. Even for lower-stakes assessments, the passing score should be set following a consideration of how the tasks as a whole represent the level of performance required to show mastery of the competency.

Role of Formative and
Summative Assessment in CBE

Assessment developers and users often refer to assessments as either **formative** or **summative**. A review of these two common assessment terms is provided below.

Formative Assessment	Summative Assessment
A process in which evidence of students' achievement or progress is used by teachers to adjust their ongoing instructional procedures or by students to adjust their current learning tactics (Good, 2011, p. 2). • Takes place *during* a period of instruction. • The results are used to adjust teaching and learning tactics.	Consists of measures that provide direct evidence of student learning outcome achievement, mastery, and competence at the end of a period of instruction or program. Learning outcomes include student knowledge, skills, competencies, attitudes and habits of mind (Suskie, 2009, p. 23). • Introduced *after* the instruction or program has concluded. • Results are used to inform decisions about the awarding of credit, credentials, and other "high stakes" student outcomes.

Figure 3. Formative and Summative Assessment

Validity and Reliability
in Formative Assessment

While general concerns about validity and reliability pertain to any assessment situation, unique issues apply to formative and summative assessments in a CBE context. Formative assessments must be administered with results available in a timely manner to enable teachers and students to benefit from the data and improve learning. To be effective, formative assessments should produce information about student learning outcomes that is easily understood and applied by faculty and students. Formative assessment results should be personalized and relevant to all students based on their knowledge, skill, and competence levels; should feature question types that are clearly linked to the curriculum and learning resources; and should be rapidly administered and scored.

While it is important that formative assessments produce consistent and stable results, the length of formative assessments should be determined based on the amount of curriculum and learning activity content that must be assessed to obtain an accurate estimate of a student's competency level on a discrete component of the course or program. Because formative assessments are frequently administered more often and in a more targeted manner than summative assessments, issues of reliability and validity are less significant, and the consequences of an error in the prediction of competence are less consequential.

In many CBE formative assessment situations, several brief formative assessments are administered throughout the program at specific curriculum milestones. While the stability of results from any single formative assessment would be unacceptable for making final decisions about competency attainment, the strategy of giving frequent short assessments is appropriate for giving immediate feedback. This strategy also supports the use of multiple assessment formats to ensure that relevant knowledge, skills, aptitudes, and competencies are measured.

Validity and Reliability in Summative Assessment

The primary objective of summative assessment in a CBE context is to reach decisions about the level of student achievement of knowledge, skills, abilities, and competencies after a period of instruction and learning. In virtually all CBE summative assessment situations, the goal is to obtain a precise and stable estimate of student achievement at a discrete time, and to use this estimate to inform decisions about student status (e.g., earns college credit, receives degree, and achieves job readiness). Although summative assessment data may be helpful in informing instructional and curriculum decision, its primary use is to determine competence. Providing feedback to students on specific aspects of their performance may not be possible, if the integrity of the assessment content needs to be protected. It is important for students and faculty alike to be aware that detailed feedback from summative assessments should not be an expectation—that is what formative assessments are for.

Due to these significant consequences, summative assessments are subject to some unique validity and reliability threats. For example, issues relating to the security and confidentiality of assessment content and student responses must be addressed. Advance access to assessment material by students and teachers would render invalid the results of even the most rigorous summative assessment. For this reason, in many summative assessment programs, a third party entity is engaged to administer and proctor assessments to ensure the integrity of the results. Further, it is considered best practice to publish sample assessments with explanations of how the assessments are administered and scored, and to make these sample guides freely available to students, teachers, and the public.

To be effective, then, summative assessments must be closely aligned with the student learning outcomes determined for a CBE program, and the scoring and reporting of summative assessment results must be carefully planned in order to support the goal of the CBE program. From an assessment development perspective, summative assessments require high levels of accuracy and precision to support inferences about students' competency levels. Depending on the nature of the CBE program, summative assessments may be very resource intensive, requiring days of separate assessment periods in order to measure all of the defined knowledge, skills, abilities, and competencies. In addition, many summative assessment developers and users apply rubrics to student assessment responses to reach decisions about competency status. Some also conduct standard-setting studies to define the expected competency level associated with varying levels of student performance. The information gained from rubric development and standard setting projects can be modified for use on score reports provided to students and other stakeholders to highlight students' learning outcome levels relative to the knowledge, skills, abilities, and competencies measured. It is important that score reports be constructed and formatted to promote broad and consistent understanding of the results, and to highlight any limitations or cautions associated with the results.

All CBE assessment, formative and summative, can benefit from the Plan-Review-Align process discussed earlier, and from documentation of assessment purpose, content, and required performance levels. While it is not feasible to invest the same resources in formative as summative exams, typically it is worthwhile to ensure that all assessment designers take to heart the basic ideas behind Plan-Review-Align, and think through and document what decisions they will make based on the assessment results. Thinking of assessment in terms of evidence for a decision, and using that awareness as the basis for all design and implementation, keeps CBE assessment grounded in its essential goal: to provide a firm foundation for the program.

References

American Educational Research Association, American Psychological Association, & National Council on Measurement in Education. (2014). *Standards for educational and psychological testing.* Washington, DC: American Psychological Association.

Downing, S. (2003). Validity: On the meaningful interpretation of assessment data. *Medical Education, 37,* 830–837. Retrieved from http://www.wiser.pitt.edu/sites/wiser/research/extra_docs/downing2003validity-onmeaningful.pdf

Epstein, R. M. (2007). Assessment in medical education. *The New England Journal of Medicine, 356,* p. 387–396. Retrieved from http://www.nejm.org/doi/full/10.1056/nejmra054784

Good, R. (2011). Formative use of assessment information: It's a process, so let's say what we mean. *Practical Assessment, Research & Evaluation, 16*(3). Retrieved from http://pareonline.net/getvn.asp?v=16&n=3

McClarty, K. & Gaertner, M. (2015). *Measuring mastery: Best practices for assessment in competency-based education.* Retrieved from http://www.aei.org/publication/measuring-mastery-best-practices-for-assessment-in-competency-based-education/

Suskie, L. (2009). *Assessing student learning: A common sense guide* (2nd ed.). San Francisco, CA: Jossey-Bass.

Chapter 3

Assessment in Action

The Clinical Performance in
Nursing Examination at Excelsior College

Mary Lee Pollard

Dean of the School of Nursing

There are arguably few educational programs in the country offering a true measure of student competency—an application of skills, knowledge, and abilities in any given field. The Clinical Performance in Nursing Examination (CPNE), created in 1970 by a group of nursing faculty experts in Albany, NY, provides an example of a clinical performance examination that allows students to demonstrate the psychomotor skills necessary for practice as a registered nurse. The CPNE has been refined over the years, but it remains the clinical capstone examination for Excelsior College's associate degree in nursing program. The lessons learned from the creation of a truly competency-based assessment are likely to be transferable to other content areas and help to illustrate the importance of aligning the assessment of competencies with sound psychometric principles.

Guiding Questions

Five essential questions help to develop a performance assessment:

1. What are the core competencies to be assessed?
2. What are the indicators that define those competencies?
3. What are the most effective ways to learn those competencies?
4. What are the most effective ways to document learners have achieved the required competencies?
5. What are the desired learner outcomes for the competency-based assessment? (Lenburg, 1979)

These questions served as the organizing framework for developing the CPNE in 1970 and continue to guide a new generation of Excelsior College faculty members in the continuous refinement of the performance examination. The following is a guide for developing a competency-based performance assessment with examples from the development of the CPNE.

What Are the Core Competencies to Be Assessed?

When developing a competency-based performance exam, the faculty or subject matter experts must identify the core competencies and skills essential for entry into practice. For the CPNE, the core competencies define nursing practice for the graduates of the program, and therefore must be applicable to a variety of practice settings as well as a patient population of all ages. Examples of the core competency areas for the CPNE include Overriding Areas of Care, Required Areas of Care, and Selected Areas of Care.

The faculty must utilize resources that are accurate and respected within the practice discipline in determining the competencies to be assessed. In this case, the CPNE subcommittee, consisting of nursing faculty and clinical experts, review the core competencies and all elements of the CPNE annually for currency and adherence with national practice standards. They utilize contemporary resources such as the *Outcomes and Competencies for Graduates of Practical/Vocational, Diploma, Associate Degree, Baccalaureate, Master's Practice Doctorate, and Research Doctorate Programs in Nursing* (National League for Nursing, 2010) and the National Council of State Boards of Nursing (2012) *RN Practice Analysis: Linking the NCLEX-RN Examination to Practice* to revise the examination as necessary.

What Are the Indicators That Define Those Competencies?

The faculty must next identify those behaviors that are mandatory for demonstration of each identified competence. This requires developing clear, unambiguous statements describing the skills required to demonstrate each competency. At Excelsior College, these statements are referred to as *critical elements*. As stated in the CPNE Study Guide (2014), the Excelsior faculty defines critical elements as "single, discrete, observable behaviors" used in measuring the student's performance.

For example, Areas of Care represent elements of nursing practice that are common across practice settings and applicable for all patients across the life span. They are considered the necessary competencies for entry into practice as a graduate of an associate degree program. Critical elements are the skills that must be accomplished to demonstrate competence in a specific Area of Care. Critical elements represent single, discrete, observable behaviors. It is essential that each critical element begin with a verb that clearly identifies the mandatory aspect of the skill to be demonstrated. The critical elements should be written in language that is clear, precise, unambiguous, and utilizes universally accepted terminology because they will be the standard by which student performance is graded. This is very important because the grading tool must be interpreted in the same manner by all examiners.

Example: In the Area of Care: Abdominal Assessment, the critical elements are as follows:

1. Complies with established guidelines.

2. Positions the patient to facilitate abdominal assessment.

3. Inspects for distention.

4. Auscultates for bowel sounds over all four (4) quadrants.

5. Performs *light* palpation over all four (4) quadrants for tenderness or rigidity, unless contraindicated.

6. Records data related to

   • distention,

   • presence or absence of bowel sounds in each of the four (4) quadrants, and

   • tenderness or rigidity.

In a performance examination, the critical elements define the actions that represent the minimum accepted level of competence. The critical elements should not include behaviors or actions that go beyond the minimum standard; only those actions or behaviors that are essential for documenting the competence should be included. For example, in the Overriding Area of Care: Care, a student is required to introduce him/herself as a minimum requirement; if a student engages in further conversation with the patient to show care or build rapport, no additional points are given because a judgment would be too subjective. In the CPNE, the critical elements represent the actions the student must perform to demonstrate the minimal level of competence for entry into practice as a registered nurse.

What Are the Most Effective Ways to Learn Those Competencies?

In a competency-based curriculum, the focus is on the outcome of student learning rather than on rule-bound processes of instruction. This idea points to one of the most significant challenges to the adoption of a competency-based program: the changing role of faculty. Traditional mandated classroom seat time, lecture, rote memorization, and required reading have proven ineffective in assisting students to demonstrate competence or significant learning.

Therefore, faculty members in a CBE environment must relinquish their role as "sage on the stage" and dispenser of wisdom. To be effective, faculty must communicate to students what skills they need to learn in order to demonstrate the desired competencies, and then assist them with their learning. The students must then abandon their passive role as classroom observer and assume an active role in their learning.

The Excelsior College nursing faculty ascribes to Malcolm Knowles's (1977) learner-centered principles of andragogy in assisting post-traditional students to prepare for the CPNE. The following assumptions inform teaching strategies:

1. Adults tend to be self-directing.

2. Adults have a richer reservoir of experience that can serve as a resource for learning.

3. Since adults' readiness to learn is frequently affected by their need to know or do something, they tend to have a life-, task-, or problem-centered orientation to learning, as contrasted to a subject-matter orientation.

4. Adults are generally motivated to learn due to internal or intrinsic factors as opposed to external or extrinsic forces. (Knowles, 1984)

At Excelsior, faculty members serve as facilitators of student learning. Their role is to clarify concepts, provide opportunities for students to practice and apply new skills, assist in accessing learning resources, and design learning resources that appeal to all learning styles. Faculty also play a critical role in assessment, which will be discussed in more detail below.

Students preparing for the CPNE are provided with a study guide containing a thorough description of each competency and critical element on which they will be tested. They are expected to learn the critical elements by practicing in their clinical practice settings (within their scope of practice); by practicing in simulated clinical environments; by reviewing faculty-developed learning resources such as videos, case studies, critical thinking exercises; and by accessing resources available from the college library. Students may also participate in phone calls with faculty; in-person, faculty-facilitated clinical skills workshops; and online conferences focusing on skills, documentation, and developing nursing care plans. The faculty and students share ownership of the learning outcomes; the students assume responsibility for their learning, and the faculty assumes responsibility for providing appropriate resources for that learning.

What Are the Most Effective Ways to Document that Learners Have Achieved the Required Competencies?

Development of a competency-based performance examination employs the same psychometric principles as a written assessment of competencies or proficiencies. In particular, a competency-based examination of any kind is criterion-referenced. This means that students must perform at an established level of performance to demonstrate a predetermined minimum accepted standard or competency. The CPNE takes a non-compensatory approach to defining minimum accepted standards: students must perform all mandatory skills at the required performance level. For each competency tested, the student must perform the required skills exactly as written. Failure to perform the skills correctly or omission of a skill represents a failure to demonstrate the competency, and therefore failure of the examination. In the CPNE, the established performance level for the exam is the level of competency of a newly graduated nurse, as determined by the faculty experts.

The psychometric concepts of objectivity, sampling, comparability, and systematized conditions guide the development and implementation of a performance assessment (Lenburg, Klein, Abdur-Rahman, Spencer, & Boyer, 2009). The most effective way to assure that these psychometric concepts are maintained and the performance examination is successful in achieving the desired measurement, is to establish protocols for administration and grading of the examination, and to insist on faculty adherence to the protocols.

Well-written examination protocols assist in maintaining objectivity in test administration and grading. The protocols guide examiner decision-making in all phases of the performance examination. They reduce faculty bias and interference from sources outside the immediate student-faculty testing situation, and they also provide guidelines for faculty to make pass-fail decisions. During the CPNE, all personal, demographic, and academic information about the student is blinded, and a different examiner is assigned to grade each new student patient-care situation (Yarbrough et al., 2007). In addition, clinical examiners are not aware of students' clinical experience or past CPNE attempts. As noted in the previous chapter, this precaution maintains objectivity and reduces bias.

Standardized sampling techniques are an efficient means for conducting a performance examination when there are multiple competencies to assess. At the start of the examination, students should be prepared to perform all of the skills essential for demonstrating the required competencies. Instead of actually requiring them to demonstrate all desired competencies, it is much more efficient to have them perform the required skills for a select sampling of competencies during the exam. They should not know until the start of the exam which ones they will be assigned. By using a protocol-driven sampling technique, the number of competencies can be reduced to a manageable number for each situation, with different competencies assigned for each testing situation. During the CPNE, the patient's needs and protocols guide faculty development of the patient care situation (PCS) assignment. By utilizing multiple patient care units in an acute care hospital, and a variety of patients at different times in the day, it is possible for a student to demonstrate a large sample of the required competencies during the testing period.

Examination protocols also ensure the standard of comparability. Each exam must be equivalent to all others in terms of level of difficulty and competencies tested. There should be little variation from one testing situation to the next. Examination protocols delineate specific standards in testing situations to assure comparable testing conditions for all students. In the CPNE, the protocols dictate (a) how patients are to be selected for testing, (b) how the assignments are determined, (c) the way in which clinical faculty and students interact during each phase of the examination, and (d) the criteria for scoring the examination. The examination protocols also provide direction for clinical examiners in seeking guidance from the exam administrator regarding student progress in performing critical elements (Lenburg, 1979; Yarbrough et al., 2007).

The examination protocols also serve to establish systematized testing conditions. The testing environment and test process, including documents, student-faculty interaction, and equipment, should not introduce bias or interfere with the examination process. In the CPNE, student-faculty interaction is scripted, and the examination documentation consists of a standardized patient care assignment form. All students receive an orientation to the patient care area and the equipment they will use during each PCS. The clinical examiner is responsible for assuring that students are provided with the necessary information and materials they will need to perform the assigned critical elements. All students are provided with the CPNE Study Guide, which essentially provides the examination blueprint, with a list of every competence and related critical elements they are responsible for learning along with the scoring tool used by the evaluating faculty.

During the CPNE, students must clearly demonstrate the ability to integrate nursing knowledge, make patient-centered judgments, and perform the technical care required for both adults and children. The examination is administered over a 2-1/2-day period in acute care hospitals located across the country. The faculty-to-student ratio is 1:1 at all times during the examination.

There are two assessment components in the CPNE: the Nursing Skills Lab (NSL) and the Patient Care Situation (PCS). The NSL consists of four stations: wound management, IV Medications: Mini

Bag, IV Medications: IV Push Meds and Injectable Medications: IM/ SQ. The student must pass all four stations with 100% accuracy; if the student fails any station they have the opportunity to have their performance assessed again on the second day of the exam. Failure on a second attempt at any of the NSL stations results in failure of the entire examination.

Students must also pass three PCSs over the course of the 2½-day testing period. Two of the PCSs must be adults and one must be a child. It is possible for a student to attempt five PCSs; they are provided the opportunity to repeat one failed adult PCS and one failed child PCS. In each PCS, the examiner provides the student with basic information about the assigned patient along with the student's assigned Areas of Care. The student then develops a nursing care plan and implements the plan of care along with the nursing behaviors associated with the assigned Areas of Care. The student is then responsible for documenting the care provided and completing the evaluation phase of their nursing care plan.

The faculty responsible for administering the CPNE assume two different roles: the role of Clinical Examiner (CE) and Clinical Associate (CA). In accordance with the standards of the American Educational Research Association, the American Psychological Association, and the National Council of Measurement in Education (referred to as AERA/ APA/NCME Standards), each new CE undergoes rigorous training on principles of performance assessment as well as examination administration and scoring protocols. They are not allowed to administer the examination with actual students until they have demonstrated complete understanding of the structure and process of the performance examination as well as mastery of administration and scoring protocols. The CE training also addresses controlling bias and maximizing equitable treatment during examination administration and scoring. The primary role of the Clinical Examiner (CE) is to act as a silent observer while scoring the student's performance on the critical elements through all phases of the examination. The CE adheres to all examination administration and scoring protocols and selects patients and creates assignments in accordance with the protocols. The CE will terminate the

Patient Care Situation (PCS) if the student fails to accurately perform a critical element. However, the CA is consulted when a point of failure is identified and before the failure is called. The Clinical Associate (CA) is responsible for coordinating, supervising, and administering the examination. The primary role of the CA is to ensure that the CPNE is conducted in a manner consistent with examination protocols. The CA also maintains security of examination materials as well as personal and demographic information about each student. Consulting the CA assures there is always a second, on-the-spot opportunity to compare the student's behavior to the scoring criteria in cases where a failure is to be declared. CAs and CEs are required to have a minimum of a master's degree in nursing, three to five years of teaching experience, and a license to practice nursing in the state in which the examination is conducted.

The criteria for selecting CPNE test sites include specifications related to the number, type, and acuity of patients admitted to the hospital. For example, there must be sufficient numbers of pediatric patients to provide the opportunity for Child Patient Care Situations required by the CPNE. All CPNE test sites must provide the opportunity for students to demonstrate nursing care across the lifespan.

What Are the Desired Learner Outcomes for This Competency-Based Assessment?

It is important to write competency-based outcomes as practice-based rather than as traditional learning objectives. Avoid use of verbs such as discuss, list, describe, recognize, and demonstrate. These verbs suggest ways of learning, rather than identifying actions the student will take as a result of learning (Lenburg et al., 2009). Competency-based outcomes must address what the learner is expected to be able to do in cognitive, affective, or psychomotor performance as a result of their learning. Learner outcomes for a competency-based performance assessment should be worded as practice expectations. The learner outcomes should be developed at the same time that the mandated competencies and related skills are identified. The learner outcomes should drive the development of learning resources and the performance assessment, and not the reverse.

All students must achieve the learner outcomes for the CPNE in order to graduate from the Excelsior College associate's degree program in nursing. The CPNE requires students to demonstrate specific competencies consistent with entry into practice as a newly graduated registered nurse. These competencies are demonstrated during the Nursing Skills Laboratory (NSL) and the PCS:

- Provide safe, quality care using nursing judgment substantiated by evidence-based standards of care.

- Apply therapeutic communication skills to establish a caring relationship with adult or pediatric patients.

- Demonstrate competency in performance of selected psychomotor skills. Use the nursing process to:

  - formulate nursing diagnoses consistent with assessment data, patients' responses to health problems, and nursing science;

  - create a plan of care that includes assessments, measureable outcomes, and interventions related to nursing diagnoses that are based on the patient's current clinical condition;

  - implement planned nursing interventions for adult and pediatric patients; and

  - evaluate the accuracy and effectiveness of the plan of care based on clinical data, nursing science and evidence-based practice.

Conclusion

The CPNE has served as the clinical capstone for the associate's degree program in nursing for 40 years, and it epitomizes the college's motto:

"What you know is more important than where or how you learned it." Little has changed in the design and administration of the CPNE. The required competencies and critical elements have evolved with advances in nursing science, but the exam administration is still guided by the psychometric principles of objectivity, sampling, comparability, and systematized conditions, and operationalized by well-established examination protocols. Improvements have been made in access and diversity of student learning resources, but students are still responsible for their learning. Nearly 50,000 students have successfully completed the program, and the clinical performance of the graduates who have completed the CPNE has been identified as comparable to or better than graduates of traditional associate degree programs (Darrah & Humbert, 2009; Gwatkin & Hancock, 2009).

References

Clinical performance in nursing examination study guide (21st ed.). (2014). Albany, NY: Excelsior College.

Darrah, M., & Humbert, R. (2009). *Excelsior College final evaluation report.* Grafton, WV: ProEvaluators, LLC.

Gwatkin, L., Hancock, M., & Javitz, H. (2009). *As well prepared, and often better: Surveying the work performance of Excelsior College associate degree in nursing graduates.* SRI Final Report for Excelsior College. Available at https://www.excelsior.edu/Excelsior_College/Publications/Work_Performance_of_Excelsior_Associate_Nursing_Graduates.pdf

Knowles, M.S. (1977). *The modern practice of adult education: Andragogy vs. pedagogy.* New York, NY: Association Press.

Knowles, M.S. (1984). Introduction: The art and science of helping adults learn. In *Andragogy in action: Applying modern principles of adult learning.* San Francisco, CA: Jossey-Bass.

Laitinen, A. (2012, September 2012). *Cracking the credit hour.* New America Foundation. Retrieved from https://static.newamerica.org/attachments/2334-cracking-the-credit-hour/Cracking_the_Credit_Hour_Sept5_0.ab0048b12824428cba568ca359017ba9.pdf/

Lenburg, C. B. (1979). *The clinical performance examination: Development and implementation.* New York, NY: Appleton-Century-Crofts.

Lenburg, C. B., Klein, C., Abdur-Rahman, V., Spencer, T., & Boyer, S. (2009, September/October). The COPA model: A comprehensive framework designed to promote quality care and competency for patient safety. *Nursing Education Perspectives, (30)*5, 312–316.

National Council of State Boards of Nursing. (2012). *RN Practice Analysis: Linking the NCLEX-RN Examination to Practice.* Chicago, IL: Author.

National League for Nursing. (2010). *Outcomes and competencies for graduates of practical/vocational, associate degree, baccalaureate, master's, practice doctorate, and research doctorate programs in nursing.* Washington, DC: National League for Nursing.

Yarbrough, S., Jones, P., Nagelsmith, L., Kim, Y., Snead, C., & Odondi, M. (2007). *Clinical performance in nursing examination technical manual: Sources of validity evidence and threats.* Albany, New York: Excelsior College.

Chapter 4

A New Competency-Based Degree
Bachelor of Science in Business

Robin Berenson

Former Associate Dean of Business

Scott Dolan

Executive Director of Accreditation, Assessment, and Strategy

Karl Lawrence

Dean of the School of Business and Technology

Introduction

As noted earlier, Excelsior College has a long history of developing innovative solutions focused on high-quality yet affordable higher educational opportunities for its primarily working-adult population. Building on the success of the competency approach used in nursing, in 2014, Excelsior's School of Business and Technology (SBT) began the development of a model that could provide students with a competency-based pathway to an undergraduate degree in business.

It became obvious rather quickly that an approach to competency-based assessment in business would be very different than one in a clinical field such as nursing. Without prescribed and standardized competencies on which to base a performance based assessment, SBT needed to rely on direct involvement from business and industry in both creating the program competencies and the culminating assessment or capstone experience. Further, the SBT program, which has historically relied on a more traditional approach to course based assessment, offers another way of looking at CBE even within the same institution. Therefore, this chapter will focus more on the program development in its entirely rather than the psychometric principles surrounding the capstone assessment. Nevertheless, a common thread links the nursing and business program: the importance of assessment in a competency-based environment.

With funding and support provided by The Bill & Melinda Gates Foundation's Next Generation Learning Challenges Breakthrough Models Incubator program, SBT set a goal to develop a competency-based program that:

1) leverages the college's long history with competency-based education, prior learning assessment, and credit aggregation;

2) enhances involvement of industry in program design, delivery, and evaluation to ensure that the program is aligned with workforce needs;

3) ensures that students who graduate from the program are able to demonstrate and evaluate their level of achievement of key competencies;

4) provides students with flexibility to complete their degree; and

5) offers students a system of support services that are delivered to those who need them, when they need them.

In its approach, SBT heeded leadership's advice to start small, with the recognition that small steps were needed in order to build something larger. The five pillars identified above guided the approach, design, and implementation of the SBT competency-based Bachelor of Science in Business (BSB) degree program.

What Are the Competencies to be Assessed?
What Are the Indicators that Define the Competencies?

As pointed out, it is important to note some key differences between the CBE model employed for the BSB program and that of the School of Nursing. One clear differentiator is the enhanced intentionality and scale of collaborations with industry. While the nursing program must meet specified standards of care in the field to meet professional licensure requirements, the competencies for a business degree are not as clearly defined or agreed upon. While the college's business degree programs have always utilized an Industrial Advisory Committee to provide input into program development, the CBE model necessitates more systematic conversations focused on the needs of employers and students. As such, corporate and industrial partners have played a central role in competency development, program and course design, program review, and end-state determinations. This chapter will look at the ways industry and employers play a role in creating this degree pathway.

Initially, it was critical that SBT prepare students to become business managers and leaders by putting special emphasis on developing the knowledge, skills, attitudes, and values needed to meet the demands of the twenty-first century workforce. A variety of strategies were used to explore employer needs, beginning with input from the Industrial Advisory Committee, which includes executive-level human resource and industry representatives in the fields of energy, utilities, health and human services, and logistics. In addition to their input, three approaches guided the faculty's development of end-state competencies:

1) a review of literature on workforce needs and the skills gap,

2) an examination of other competency-based models (i.e. the Department of Labor's Competency-Model Clearinghouse), and

3) in-depth reviews of job databases like O*NET online, which contains information on the knowledge, skills, and abilities of hundreds of occupations based on surveys of a broad range of workers.

Based on this input, the faculty developed a draft list of program-level competencies in essential business knowledge, professional skills, and behaviors. For feedback, the list was reviewed by both employers and industry groups. Meetings with members from industry partners—as diverse as CSX (transportation) and Yum! Brands (a Fortune 500 fast food corporation)—as well as meetings with representatives from the U.S. Chamber of Commerce, helped solidify a final list of 15 program-level core competencies that formed the framework for the subsequent development of the program. The competencies, listed below, are geared toward providing students with a foundational knowledge of business administration and strategic management. In all instances, because of the CBE's emphasis on workplace-valued outcomes, it was important to develop competencies that focused on content mastery, as well as the ability to apply knowledge in practice.

- **Economics:** Apply modern micro- and macroeconomic concepts and theories to explain the relationship between the legal, social, and economic interests of individuals and society.

- **Accounting:** Apply basic accounting concepts and principles to the analysis and interpretation of corporate financial statements.

- **Marketing:** Explain how modern marketing concepts and theories support and influence business strategies.

- **Finance:** Utilize financial management concepts and tools in order to make informed business decisions.

- **Management:** Apply the major concepts and theories of management and leadership in order to develop business strategies in a real-world context.

- **Quantitative Analysis:** Utilize quantitative research, statistics, and data analysis to analyze business data, support business decisions, and solve problems.

- **Global:** Analyze the opportunities and risks associated with doing business in a global environment.

- **Ethics:** Justify decisions by evaluating the social, ethical, and legal implications for business organizations.

- **Communication:** Effectively communicate business concepts orally and in writing to multiple audiences.

- **Computer Skills:** Utilize business computer applications and information technologies to organize and interpret business data and information.

- **Teamwork/Cultural Diversity:** Work effectively and collaboratively on diverse teams to complete projects based on real-world scenarios.

- **Critical Thinking:** Employ critical thinking skills to interpret and analyze competing arguments and perspectives in a business environment.

- **Leadership:** Organize tasks and understand how to delegate responsibility in order to complete collaborative projects in a timely manner.

- **Lifelong Learning:** Evaluate their individual strengths and weaknesses with the desire to update skills and continuously improve.

- **Business Strategy:** Apply knowledge of business concepts and functions in an integrated manner in order to make strategic decisions in a real-world context.

The competency development stage posed some challenges because of the wide variety of career paths open to students who graduate with a degree in business. Thus, the process of honing in on specific competencies that could apply across all industries and work contexts became difficult. This stands in contrast to the nursing program, where proscribed competencies are more easily identified because the field is standardized by licensure requirements.

Despite the challenge of identifying specific competencies, it became clear that there were key competencies expected of new employees in basic business knowledge and skills from the core discipline areas of economics, accounting, finance, and marketing. Such in-demand competencies included

- proficiency with quantitative analysis,

- proficiency in oral and written communication,

- proficiency with computer applications,

- ability to adapt to the rapidly changing and globalizing workplace,

- ability to learn new knowledge and skills while on the job, and

- ability to work on and lead culturally diverse teams.

In addition, SBT added behavior areas of competency such as lifelong learning, leadership, and teamwork for future development.

Program and Course Design

The involvement of industry did not end with the development of program-level competencies, but also included curriculum and course design, most notably in the development of a capstone course for the program. Excelsior College considers a capstone course a culmination of the program that integrates components of the program and gives students an opportunity to demonstrate achievement of learning goals. Industry representatives helped create performance expectations within the capstone, used to assess whether students have demonstrated sufficient achievement of program competencies. Furthermore, industry representatives with expertise in accounting, finance, marketing, operations, management, and business strategy acted as the primary subject-matter experts in the creation of learning modules for the capstone simulation. Finally, employers played a key role in the development of a final project within the capstone course, a team-based, entrepreneurial business plan. Employers reviewed and provided input into the analytical rubric that will be used to assess student work at multiple points.

Since industry representatives have been at the table throughout the program review process, and have played a role in building student, alumni and supervisor surveys, Excelsior's corporate partners and potential employers are able to better validate the success of programs. Most importantly, the program utilizes industry representatives in its individual outcome determination, and in an audit of the full program. In so doing, the continuous quality improvement process for the program is maintained to ensure that student learning meets evolving expectations.

What Are the Most Effective Ways to Document Learners Have Achieved Required Competencies?

Because employers have expressed concerns with the preparedness of college graduates for the workplace, SBT began this CBE program with the intent of creating a way for students to demonstrate attainment of real, work-force competencies at the time of graduation. Thus, the focus was on developing an integrated learning experience that would enable students to be **ADEPT**:

Apply their content knowledge;

Develop an appreciation for lifelong learning;

Evaluate their individual strengths and weaknesses;

Practice key professional skills; and

Translate their learning experience into a personalized pathways for success.

To help students become ADEPT, the capstone includes a collaborative mentoring process that helps students identify their strengths and weaknesses on each of the fifteen competencies. Using this information, students develop an action plan within the 15-week capstone course to address their challenges and opportunities. While the program does not require that all students master all competencies, as is expected in the CPNE, the program does expect that students will enhance their self-knowledge in all areas, and then use this self-knowledge to update their overall competency.

Thus, the capstone course developed for the Bachelor of Science in Business program is designed to allow students to demonstrate the required competencies. It is a six-credit, fifteen-week culminating experience required for all students within the program. While taking the course, students are given the opportunity to demonstrate competencies to faculty and industry experts through a variety of assessments, including

- multiple choice exams assessing students' business content knowledge;

- behavioral assessments designed to help students understand their own behaviors;

- simulations focused on application of business knowledge to real-world contexts; and

- a team-based entrepreneurial business plan designed to integrate competencies and assess a student's ability to develop business strategies.

The capstone is divided into three phases; each phase builds on the last in an effort to scaffold a student's learning and culminate in an authentic application of knowledge, skills and abilities. The capstone phases are:

1) foundation,

2) practice, and

3) application.

During each phase, learning is supported so that students are able to address their unique strengths and weaknesses. Such a personalized approach enables students to interact with faculty and move towards greater independence. Following is a closer look at each of these three stages, their implementation, time required, and achievement goals of each.

1. Foundation Stage (pre-assessment and content; two weeks)

During the foundation stage, students take an internally developed, criterion-referenced pre-assessment (i.e., multiple choice set of exams) focused on their knowledge and understanding of business theories and concepts in the following nine areas: accounting, economics, management, quantitative business analysis, computer applications, finance, marketing, and the legal and social environment. Additionally, students are asked to participate in a suite of behavioral self-assessments to establish baseline data for behavioral competencies (e.g., interpersonal workplace behaviors, communication, teamwork, and leadership). The behavioral self-assessment tool, called the DISCFLEX™, focuses on a student's behavioral profile in four areas:

- **Dominance:** relates to control, power, and assertiveness.
- **Influence**: relates to individual's approach to social situations, and style of communication.
- **Steadiness**: refers to level of patience, degree of cooperation, and dependability.
- **Compliance**: refers to a person's organization and their need for structure.

Based on the results of the content and behavioral assessments, students work with instructors on a competency mapping exercise, where they identify their individual areas of strength and weakness and develop an action plan to address shortcomings during the remainder of the capstone course and beyond. This action plan is a living document used to assess the lifelong learning component of the CBE-BSB program; this component requires students to regularly evaluate their individual strengths and weaknesses as they strive toward continuous self-improvement. In addition to a behavioral assessment, the DISCFLEX™ system can also help students with lifelong learning by directing them towards online learning resources that can support performance improvement and change or develop their behaviors in a variety of work contexts.

Components of the DISCFLEX™ system, including personalized e-learning tutorials, are embedded throughout the capstone. With e-learning tutorials that are created based on students' individual DISC assessments, activities include readings and videos, to reinforce ways to adapt their interpersonal behaviors to specific situations.

2. Practice Stage (simulation; eight weeks)

Supplementing the foundational work is a practice period involving a simulation that allows students to apply their understanding of business to scenarios that align with industry-relevant tasks. Four modules were specifically developed for the simulation and are focused on the following areas:

1) accounting and finance;

2) marketing;

3) operations and management; and

4) strategy.

The simulations ask students to play the role of a business consultant who works for a firm hired to evaluate growth opportunities for a restaurant supply and service company. Additionally, students are then asked to complete journaling exercises: small reflection papers designed to enable them to capture their thought processes, document their own perceptions of what they have learned, and strategize how decisions made within the simulation will be communicated to the company receiving the student's consulting services. To make the simulation more realistic, students are given biographical sketches of the individuals they are expected to communicate with and to think about ways their own DISC profile may affect their communication strategy. In so doing, students are provided with an opportunity to practice, applying what they have learned through their behavioral DISC self-assessments.

As part of the simulation, instructors and students have access to dashboards, enabling instructors to monitor student engagement and performance, and provide students feedback. Instructors are directed to use information on the dashboard to provide just-in-time assistance and personalized instruction. During the simulation period, students check in with instructors to revisit their competency mapping exercises, where they utilize a journaling feature within Blackboard to identify specific actions to enhance strengths or improve weaknesses.

3. Application Stage (final project, summative exam, life-long learning plan; five weeks)

In the final stage of the course, students are assigned a team-based entrepreneurial business plan project that synthesizes their learning from the entire program and applies their understanding of business theories and concepts to develop a growth strategy for the simulated organization. Teams consist of three members, and students are divided into groups based on the functional areas of business where they have identified weaknesses. The business plan is expected to be a consolidated presentation that includes elements of a typical business plan, including industry, marketing, and competitive analyses, as well as management, marketing, operations, and financial plans. In order to develop the business plan, students are expected to do additional research, as well as leverage open-educational resources found within the simulation and the course.

During the applied stage, students complete a criterion-referenced summative assessment, designed to reassess students' knowledge and understanding of core business theories and concepts, and their ability to apply such knowledge to analyze and solve problems. The same nine areas assessed in the pre-assessment during the first two weeks of the courses will be assessed at the conclusion of the course in order to determine the extent to which students have achieved program competencies in the foundational business content areas.

With the ADEPT model, SBT recognized that learning does not end with the capstone experience. To reinforce continual learning and document competency at the completion of the program, students complete a lifelong learning action plan based on their level of achievement. This map reflects their strengths and weaknesses across the different areas assessed within the capstone. It is designed to provide students with a resource that will not only document their knowledge and skills in different areas but will also map next steps for career development.

What Are the Most Effective Ways to Learn the Competencies?

Given Excelsior's history serving working adult populations, the SBT aimed to develop a program that provided students with numerous options to complete their degree and demonstrate their competency. Offering students multiple avenues, or personalized pathways, to complete degree requirements gives students the option to choose the learning experience best suited to their individual circumstances. Because students are given a number of options, the time it takes them to complete the BSB degree will vary.

Option 1: Course Option

Excelsior's online courses are available for students who want and need structure with a set start and end date (8 or 15 weeks in length), aligning with standard academic terms. Courses align with the program competencies, integrate open educational resources, and are instructor-led. Authentic and traditional assessments are used that incorporate real-life applicability and project-based learning in ways that are consistent and comparable to the capstone experience.

Option 2: Credit by Exam

Self-paced learning experiences are available for students who do not desire or need the course experience. For example, some students may have prior workplace or educational experiences that have prepared them to demonstrate competency via exams developed by the Center for Educational Measurement (CEM) at Excelsior. These exams are psychometrically-designed, criterion-referenced assessments that allow students to earn college level credit by meeting proficiency standards. They are offered in a computer-based format at test centers around the world. Students are provided with guides to prepare for the exams and are directed to open-education resources for exam preparation. Students who achieve the passing level of performance on the exam are granted college credit.

Option 3: Earned External Credits

Students have the option to transfer credit from other institutions or earn credit for prior learning/workplace training while enrolled as students at the college. Success is assessed through three approaches, depending on the source: prior learning assessment portfolios, workplace training mapped to college degree programs through the Center for the Assessment of Post-Traditional Instruction, Training, and Learning (CAPITAL), and evaluated credit transferred from accredited and nonaccredited institutions.

More importantly, as noted with the development of the nursing program and assessments, students, especially adult learners in a CBE environment, need specialized services; therefore, the exploration of a competency-based education model for the BSB program required a deeper look at how student services might best be delivered in a CBE environment, ensuring that support services are provided by the college and not wholly a responsibility of the business department. Traditionally at the college, student support was provided by an individual instructor or school-based academic advisors. With the integrated model, the goal is to collaborate across the college to increase student awareness about the array of resources available and to match students to the specific resources they require. To that end, some key changes are being considered in order to improve the delivery of student support:

1. **Targeted academic advising that combines degree completion planning, student services, and career planning with a goal of stacking credentials (degree plus certification) when possible.** Advisors work with students to identify, recommend, and proactively coordinate appropriate student support and career services, utilizing the college's MAP (My Academic Plan) to assist students in selecting curriculum pathways that are a fit for an individual's life circumstances. Adding career and credentialing components to academic advising enables the program to emphasize the relevance of a degree while highlighting the transferability of competencies to the market.

2. **Choice in the curriculum pathway toward a degree and tools to help students make choices.** To assist advisors and students in choosing curriculum pathways, the college recently received funding from the Foundation for the Improvement of Postsecondary Education (FIPSE) to develop the Diagnostic Assessment and Achievement of College Skills (DAACS). DAACS is an open-source assessment tool that will allow colleges and universities to fit resources and services to students based on their academic (reading, writing, and math) and nonacademic (academic self-regulation, grit, math anxiety, and test anxiety) skills. The tool will be developed to provide students with

personalized learning strategies. The CBE program will be able to use the information from DAACS to target interventions based upon each student's individual need.

3. Full access to integrated support services. Excelsior has a wide array of services that are available to enrolled students at no additional cost, including its online library, online writing lab (OWL), veterans center, disabilities services, and a student ombudsperson; in addition, the college extends additional writing and tutoring services provided by external vendors such as Smarthinking, Grammarly, and Atomic Learning. Advisors and instructors are trained on the use of these resources.

4. Opportunities to interact directly with employers and industry stakeholders in an outcome-oriented context. Two-way conversations at the point of the capstone provide employers and potential employees with meaningful opportunities to collaborate, network, and connect. Students will know that they leave the program with authentic, tangible evidence of their skills and abilities.

Conclusion

While CBE program development started small, Phase II is already underway. During this phase, faculty and industry representatives have begun to redesign both the course and exam options to align with the newly developed program competencies. As new concentrations are developed, curriculum will continue to be aligned with relevant industry standards. Through the full development of the BSB program, Excelsior will continue to provide students with a high-quality, rigorous academic program that prepares students for employment *and* encourages lifelong learning; however, our program will only be successful if employers have confidence that our graduates can demonstrate the ability to apply their learning directly to the workplace. The only way to determine if our graduates can do so is through a rigorous, authentic assessment designed with input from the very employers we are seeking to serve.

Works Consulted

Arum, R., & Roksa, J. (2011). *Academically adrift*. Chicago, IL: University of Chicago Press.

CareerOneStop. (n.d.). *Competency Model Clearinghouse*. Retrieved from www.CareerOneStop.org/CompetencyModel

Carnevale, A. P., & Rose, S. J. (2015). *The economy goes to college: The hidden promise of higher education in the post-industrial service economy*. Retrieved from https://cew.georgetown.edu/wp-content/uploads/EconomyGoesTo College.pdf

Carnevale, A. P., Smith, N., & Strohl, J. (2010, June). *Projections of jobs and education requirements through 2018*. The Georgetown University: Center on Education and the Workforce. Washington, DC: Georgetown University.

Carnevale, A., Smith, N., & Strohl, J. (2013). *Recovery: Job growth and education requirements through 2020*. The Georgetown University: Center on Education and the Workforce. Washington, DC: Georgetown University.

Klein-Collins, R. (2012). *Competency-based degree programs in the U.S.* Retrieved from http://www.cael.org/pdfs/2012_competencybasedprograms

Mendenhall, R. (2012). Western Governors University. In D. G. Oblinger (Ed.), *Game changers: Education and information technology* (ch. 9). Retrieved from http://www.educause.edu/library/resources/chapter-9-western-governors-university

Person, A., Goble, L., & Bruch, J. (2014, April 30). Developing competency-based program models in three community colleges. *Mathematica Policy Research*. Retrieved from http://www.mathematica-mpr.com/~/media/publications/PDFs/education/compentency-based_program_models.pdf

Weise, M. & Christensen, C. (2014). Hire education: Mastery, modularization, and the workforce revolution. *Clayton Christensen Institute for Disruptive Innovation*. Retrieved from http://www.christenseninstitute.org/wp-content/uploads/2014/07/Hire-Education.pdf

Epilogue

Tina Goodyear

Unless you happen to be a psychometrician, assessment is not likely a favorite subject; it carries with it much controversy and threatens to challenge ideas about academic freedom and one-size-fits-all approaches to learning. Even seasoned educators are not necessarily familiar or comfortable with the principles of assessment, particularly in the case of CBE where application of skills is given more weight than the possession of knowledge in a subject area. Yet a lack of clarity, a fear of standardization, and a dearth of expertise in how to truly assess learning has brought about an interesting, and arguably disturbing, effect on higher education. We have become critical of the very system put in place to assure quality-accreditation, and have somehow stifled our nation's ability to innovate in higher education. Uncertainty surrounding assessment is likely at the crux of those issues.

If institutions could offer valid and reliable results that substantiate the level to which a student has learned and can apply learning, we would be able to rely far less on our current measures of "learning"—seat time, satisfactory academic progress, delivery methods, and substantive interaction—as a way to ensure quality. Accreditors could serve their intended role as arbiters of quality assurance, and we would have more confidence in spending federal dollars on providers and programs that produce strong evidence of actual student learning. After all, if we can assure that a student has learned what he/she needs to learn to move to the next level (employment, graduate school, etc.), and that learning can be proven to be a reliable prerequisite for success at that next level, a focus on the inputs mentioned above will be less important and perhaps all institutions, regardless of prestige or price tag, would be accountable to the same standard.

Over forty years ago, Excelsior College, like many adult-focused institutions, came up with a way to help working adults—those twenty-five and older—attain a degree by recognizing and valuing the knowledge, skills, and abilities these students already possessed upon enrollment. In order to justify this innovate approach, assessment became the bedrock of the institution. As CBE continues to grow in popularity as a promise to help bridge the skills gap, and meet aggressive college completion goals, the issue of assessment—as it is so articulately addressed in this guide—will be paramount to our nation's discourse in higher education.

Appendix

Legal Matters

John Ebersole and Mary Lee Pollard

Introduction

After 40 years of preparing ADN students for their degree, and the opportunity to sit for the National Council Licensing Examination (the NCLEX), plus the ability to track and evaluate nearly 50,000 graduates, one would assume that the CBE approach to RN licensure is established and accepted. Unfortunately, that is not always the case.

Over the past 10 years, Excelsior has been challenged in nine states by state boards that want to prevent our graduates from being licensed in their states. In each case, existing recognition has been in place for decades, and no data, research, or precipitating event has been presented to suggest a problem. In fact, national research conducted by SRI in 2009 determined that Excelsior's CBE graduates "performed as well as, or better than" those trained by more conventional programs. These findings were largely ignored because the study had been commissioned by Excelsior.

Of the nine state challenges, only California's has been successful. This, due to the strong opposition of the CBE approved by the California Nurses Association (CNA), as well as Excelsior's failure to seek resolution through the legislative process. In the other jurisdictions,

Excelsior prevailed, but only after sizeable expenditures of time and money.

As this is being written, we have been informed that the board of nursing in a large southern state is preparing, once again, to end recognition of our program because of its reliance on competency assessment, rather than traditional precepted clinical instruction. In other words, inputs continue to trump outcomes. For this reason, we present more detailed information about legal and legislative issues that might affect other institutions wishing to offer competency-based assessment in programs leading to licensure.

Case Study 1: California Board of Nursing

In 1979, the California board of nursing began licensing graduates of the Excelsior College AD program. The graduates were eligible for licensure based on the board of nursing's interpretation of California Business and Professions Code section 2736. The board recognized the AD program as "equivalent to the minimum requirements of the board for licensure established for an accredited programs in California" (Excelsior College v. California Board of Registered Nursing, 2006). The California board of nursing continued to license Excelsior graduates for more than 24 years.

In January 2003 the board of nursing education/licensing committee recommended the board cease recognition of the AD program as meeting the minimum requirements. The College attempted to work with the board of nursing to educate them on the competency assessment model, the rigor of the CPNE, and the prior clinical education and qualifications of the students enrolled in the program. The College and the board members held multiple meetings on the issue but were unable to reach an agreement that would allow the AD graduates to be licensed in California. It was the college's belief that it was within the jurisdiction of the board to continue to interpret and apply the California Business and Professions Code section 2736 in a manner that permitted them to license Excelsior graduates. The board did not agree and was adamant that the statute was clear on this matter. The College then determined it was necessary to seek a legislative remedy and hired a lobbying firm and reached out to members of the California legislature. The College's attempt for a legislative remedy was unsuccessful and in February 2003, the board made the following determination,

> Excelsior College graduates, like other out-of-state graduates, must meet the requirements set forth in California Business and Professions Code Section 2736 (a) (2) and California Code of Regulations Section 1426, including the requirement of supervised clinical practice concurrent with theory, in order to be eligible for examination and licensure as a California registered nurse. This eligibility requirement applies to students who enrolled on or after December 2003. (Excelsior College v. California Board of Registered Nursing, 2006)

The College, with the backing of the Board of Trustees, then made the decision to file suit against the California Board of Registered Nursing in December 2003. The College sought to invalidate the board's interpretation of the statute, specifically section 2736, and compel the board to continue to accept the AD program as equivalent to California's minimum requirements. The court found in favor of the board of nursing and the college filed an appeal in September 2004. In its appeal, the college alleged the board of nursing revoked its prior findings that Excelsior's AD program was equivalent to the minimum requirements without any changes in either the Excelsior program or the statute. The College also claimed that the board's adoption and implementation of the new interpretation of statutory authority denied Excelsior due process of law and caused direct injury to the college and its students. Excelsior further claimed this statutory interpretation violated the commerce clause of the United States Constitution because it imposed a discriminatory and unreasonable burden on out-of-state nursing schools as compared to in-state schools (Excelsior College v. California Board of Registered Nursing, 2006). Following briefing and oral arguments, the Court of Appeal issued its decision in favor of the board of nursing on February 26, 2006.

Until recently, the college continued to retain a lobbyist in California with the hope of establishing a means for graduates to obtain licensure; either by examination or endorsement. After years of meeting with representatives of professional nursing organizations, the hospital association, the board of nursing, and individual legislators seeking support in our effort to have Excelsior graduates licensed in California, the college was successful in having a member of the State Assembly sponsor a bill that would provide a mechanism for graduates to achieve licensure by endorsement. Unfortunately, as the bill began to gain momentum within the Assembly Business and Professions Committee, the assemblyman lost his bid for re-election in November 2014.

The College has since made the decision to end our lobbying efforts and take a wait-and-see approach, hoping that in the future the board will change its stance on mandating concurrent clinical instruction in nursing education programs. Unfortunately, there continues to be no mechanism for Excelsior graduates to obtain licensure in California. The College has lists of alumni, many of whom hold licensure in other states, and have earned advanced degrees and certifications and wish to move to California, but have been denied licensure—not based on review of their current practice, but rather based on perceived deficiencies in their education.

Case Study 2: Georgia Board of Nursing

A similar challenge to the Excelsior AD program was brought by the Georgia board of nursing. At the close of the 2008 legislative session, the Georgia board of nursing proposed a bill that was presented in public hearings as administrative "clean-up" language and an additional requirement for background investigations as part of the requirements for registered nurse licensure in Georgia. The bill was accepted without comment or dissent from members of the legislature or the professional nursing community. Once the bill was implemented, the Georgia board of nursing ended their 33 year practice of licensing graduates of the Excelsior College AD nursing program in July 2008. The denial of licensure for the Excelsior AD graduates was based on the board's interpretation of the bill, which required the board of nursing to approve out-of-state nursing programs deemed to be "substantially equivalent and no less stringent than approved in-state programs" (HB 1041). The Georgia board of nursing found Excelsior's program to be substantially equivalent but less stringent. This determination was made without consultation with representatives of the School of Nursing, and was not based on evidence of poor performance on the NCLEX-RN examination, a higher incidence of discipline for the Excelsior graduates, or feedback from employing agencies.

The College along with the leadership of the Georgia Nurses Association (GNA)—an organization with whom the college contracts to administer the CPNE in the state of Georgia—appealed to the board of nursing to request reconsideration of their determination that the program was less stringent than approved in-state programs. Efforts were made to educate the board members regarding competency-based education and the rigor of the CPNE. The appeal for reconsideration of their decision was denied by the board. The College then appealed to the secretary of state of Georgia and finally the governor. Both the secretary of state and the governor were sympathetic to our appeal but both were ineffective in influencing the board's decision. The staff of the board of nursing report to the secretary of state and the members of the board of nursing are appointed by the governor. The board chair refused the governor's request for a negotiated settlement. Following the governor's replacement of the board chair, the board's decision remained unchanged. A letter-writing campaign was then mounted with more than 3000 prospective and enrolled students as well as graduates, writing to their legislators, the governor, and the board of nursing expressed their dismay with the board's decision. Following the letter-writing campaign and media coverage, the college administration and representatives from the GNA were provided an opportunity to address the board in September 2008. The outcome of the hearing and requests for follow-up meetings resulted in continued refusals by the board of nursing to consider a compromise to their decision.

Since the board continued to refuse to work with the college to seek a compromise, the college determined the next step was to retain legal counsel. The College contracted with the former General Counsel for the Georgia Department of Education and the immediate past Executive Counsel to the Governor and the Office of the Governor. The College attorney, in collaboration with the current Counsel to the Governor, sought to engage the board of nursing in discussion around compromise, with no result. As a result, on November 14, 2008 Governor Perdue issued a press release stating, "This administration has not seen any evidence to suggest that graduates of the schools seeking approval yesterday (at a Georgia board of nursing meeting) have posed a threat to public health or safety. Further, I do not agree that recent legislation dictated the conclusion reached by the Board" (Ebersole, 2011). Within days of Governor Perdue's press release, the sponsor of HB 1041, the House Health and Human Services Committee Chairwoman Sharon Cooper, a registered nurse, convened a meeting of the state's nursing school deans and directors. Individuals in attendance reported that the deans were directed to discuss the board of nursing's position with their faculty members and to ask them to write letters to the board of nursing's executive director, the lieutenant governor, the secretary of state, the governor, the speaker of the house and members of the Health and Human Service Committee.

In November, the college published a paid "advertorial" in the *Atlanta Journal Constitution*. The quarter-page article informed readers of the restrictions being placed on Excelsior College and the School of Nursing and also raised concerns about the impact the board of nursing's decision would have on the state's health care system. The article also demonstrated to the 3000 prospective and enrolled students and graduates that the college was working to assist them (Ebersole, 2011).

In December 2008, the college counsel identified a senator willing to carry legislation (SB49) to remedy the problems caused with passage of HB 1041. The goal was to introduce the bill in the Senate and through the Higher Education Committee, and prevent it from being bottled up in the House's Health and Human Resources Committee, chaired by the original sponsor of HB 1041, Representative Cooper. Once SB49 was introduced in the House, Representative Cooper introduced her own bill, HB475—a highly restrictive bill based on a traditional and philosophical stance that there is only one way to educate nurses and it must include 800 hours of faculty supervised clinical in a hospital setting. After much back door politicking, a compromise agreement was reached and HB475 was passed in the Senate and returned to the House in an amended form for vote. The agreement required graduates to arrange for a precepted clinical experience in an acute care hospital. The bill was signed into law by Governor Perdue on April 29, 2009.

Despite the passage of the compromise legislation, a backlog of more than 100 applications for licensure for Excelsior graduates was not acted upon during the nine months following implementation of HB475. The board claimed to have inadequate resources to manage the applications while the college determined that the board was not adhering to the requirements of the law and were reviewing the applications on a case-by-case basis and deviating from the requirements outlined in the statute. Representatives of the college and their legal council met numerous times with the board of nursing staff and Representative Cooper to remedy this situation.

In March of 2010, the college and their attorney met with a group of approximately 20 Excelsior graduates who were experiencing difficulty in obtaining Georgia RN licensure. In the six months that followed that meeting, the attorney (on retainer with Excelsior) was able to assist four of those graduates in obtaining licensure. Also in the spring of 2010, the executive director of the board of nursing was replaced and a graduate of the Excelsior College AD program was appointed to the board of nursing. It is believed that the continued efforts by the college on behalf of the graduates, and the changes in the board of nursing membership, caused the board of nursing to adopt more efficient methods for processing the Excelsior College graduates' applications. During the last five years, Excelsior graduates have not experienced the delays in processing difficulty in meeting the additional requirements that graduates experienced immediately following passage of HB475.

Case Study 3: Virginia Board of Nursing

In April of 2008, new regulations governing the practice of nursing went into effect in the state of Virginia. Regulation 18 VAC 90-20-120.E states that programs preparing for licensure as a registered nurse shall provide a minimum of 500 hours of direct client care supervised by qualified faculty. The Virginia board of nursing notified Excelsior College that graduates of the AD program would no longer be eligible for licensure effective September 2008. The members of the board of nursing and executive director were open and responsive to questions from the college regarding providing a means for licensure for the Virginia residents enrolled in the program. The board determined that students enrolled at the time of the regulation change would be eligible for licensure by examination if they completed the program by December 31, 2009. The board also determined that Excelsior graduates could seek licensure by endorsement with evidence of 960 hours of RN practice in another state.

Although the board was responsive to requests from the college regarding a plan for currently enrolled students and those wishing to apply for licensure by endorsement, there were still almost 600 students remaining in the program who were left with no means of obtaining licensure in their home state following program completion. Conversations with the board of nursing suggested that a compromise might be possible but it would require a regulatory amendment. Armed with this information, the college utilized the services of a lobbyist in the

Virginia area to assess the potential for a legislative remedy for the situation. In the meantime, representatives of the college continued to meet with the board of nursing on a regular basis to enlighten them about the competency-based program, the criteria limiting admission to only individuals with clinical experience, and information about the rigor and validity of the CPNE. In July 2010 the board and representatives from the college reached an agreement in principle for a means to issue a preliminary license which would permit new graduates to work in Virginia and complete the required precepted hours. The College lobbyist assisted in gaining support for the proposal from the Governor's office and key legislators.

In May of 2011 a member of the board of nursing traveled to Albany and met with members of the faculty and nursing leadership team and observed a CPNE administration. The board member provided full report of her observations of the CPNE and her understanding of the competency-based model during the July 2011 board meeting. A representative of the college was also invited to attend the meeting and respond to questions from the board.

Finally, in August 2013 emergency regulations were approved to allow provisional licensure for Excelsior graduates. The provisional licensure provided them the opportunity to work under the direct supervision of a licensed RN and complete the mandated 500 hours of clinical practice included in the original regulations. The regulations also provided a means for Licensed Practical Nurses (LPN) to be credited with 150 hours based on their educational experiences in their LPN programs and graduates of the Excelsior program to be credited with 100 clinical hours for their CPNE experience. The emergency regulations were in effect through January 2015. The permanent regulations were approved by the legislature in September 2014 but were required to move through a review process that included the Attorney General, the Department of Planning and Budget, and the Secretary of Health and Human Resources. The review process lasted 150 days, then the regulations were published for a 60 day period of public comment. Once the comment period closed they were passed to the Governor for his signature. Unfortunately, while the regulations were on the Governor's desk, the sitting Governor's term of office ended and a new Governor was elected. The permanent regulations were signed by the Governor in July 2015.

All three board of nursing challenges were based on the interpretations of regulations by the state boards of nursing. In each instance, the college was notified by a student that the board of nursing had made a determination that they "could not" continue to license graduates of the Excelsior program. Of course, the boards of nursing in California, Georgia and Virginia have no obligation to communicate or collaborate with the New York based-Excelsior College School of Nursing regarding their new interpretation of regulations but it is also the opinion of the Excelsior leadership; that these new interpretations were purposeful and directed toward the competency-based AD program.

One of the many services provided by the NCSBN to the member boards of nursing are the monthly regional conference calls hosted by a NCSBN staff member. The College leadership is aware that during the period of time immediately before and after the NCSBN published their position paper titled, *Clinical Instruction in Prelicensure Nursing Programs* (2005) the regular monthly calls focused on the "New York program without any clinical." The NCSBN position paper suggests prelicensure nursing education programs should include supervised clinical experiences with actual patients. The paper also recommends that faculty members retain the responsibility to demonstrate that programs have clinical experiences with actual patients that are sufficient to meet program outcomes (NCSBN, 2005). The position paper also notes the authors found that "research on nursing clinical education was limited. Specifically, there was no research on the outcomes of programs that exclusively use alternatives to clinical experiences" (NCSBN, 2005, p. 3). Despite the lack of research to support the traditional model of clinical instruction, the NCSBN Delegate Assembly passed a resolution in support of the necessity for inclusion of planned, structured, supervised clinical instruction across the life-span as essential to nursing education. It is the college leadership's belief, that the position paper and the NCSBN staff person's characterization of the AD program as the "New York program with no clinical" was the impetus for the challenges to the program. There was no increase in incidence of disciplinary actions in any state, there was no change in NCLEX-RN outcomes and there was no change in accreditation.

In response to the NCSBN position paper and as a means to respond to the state board of nursing challenges, the college commissioned a white paper titled, *Clinical Education in Prelicensure Associate Degree Nursing Programs* (2009) by Dine Huber. Huber's paper serves many purposes. The paper demonstrates the lack of evidence in support of a mandate for specific number of clinical hours or a specific method or circumstance in which the students acquire the hours. It also makes the point that the nursing profession uses the NCLEX-RN examination as a means to measure competency for practice. The NCLEX-RN does not measure psychomotor ability or the ability to apply critical thinking to a clinical situation. Many state board regulations require clinical experiences in prelicensure programs, but no state boards have requirements regarding the outcomes of the experience; in essence the regulations don't mandate a specific level of performance as an outcome of the mandated experience. Excelsior graduates are required to pass the CPNE and therefore, are required to demonstrate they have successfully mastered the clinical skills necessary to practice as a RN (Huber, 2009).

The successful outcomes in Georgia and Virginia can be attributed to the persistence of the college staff in pursuing a means for licensure for the students and graduates caught in the middle of these philosophical differences. Although both challenges ended with a legislative remedy, the actual process was very different. From the start, there was very little collegial communication between the Georgia board of nursing and the Excelsior staff. Many letters went unanswered and requests to appear before the board of nursing were denied. Meetings with the board and Representative Cooper were often contentious with representatives from the college being banned from Representative Cooper's office. The College later learned that our alliance with the Georgia Nurses Association may have contributed to the acrimony but this was never expressed in the few productive conversations with the board of nursing or Representative Cooper. In Georgia, there was no progress toward a resolution until the college employed a well-connected lobbyist and attorney and new appointments were made to the board of nursing.

In contrast, the college's experience with the Virginia board of nursing was collegial and responsive. The College was permitted opportunities to address the board of nursing and a board member visited the college and observed the CPNE. Despite philosophical differences in beliefs about nursing education, the board was willing to work with the college and our lobbyist in reaching an acceptable resolution.

There are lessons to be learned from the challenges with the state boards. Most importantly is the need to retain open dialog with the boards of nursing whenever possible. This would encourage communication regarding proposed rule changes prior to implementation and perhaps collaboration and a mutually beneficial outcome. There are many ways to promote an open dialog with state boards. Most executive directors and board of nursing presidents attend the annual NCSBN meeting. This meeting is open to outside agencies and there is opportunity for networking and meeting with the representatives from each state. It is also an opportunity to learn about new initiatives, regulatory concerns and research being conducted by the NCSBN.

Another method to keep an open dialog with state boards is to provide information about the program on a regular basis. The membership of the each state board changes annually and therefore, it is important to provide frequent information regarding the program graduates' performance such as achievement of program outcomes and especially employer satisfaction. One means for keeping a board of nursing and other stakeholder groups updated is to send information regarding achievement of program outcomes. The results of the Excelsior College exit, one-year and three-year alumni surveys are published on the college website each year. These reports also include the information collected from graduates' employers regarding their performance one-year following program completion. This information can also be shared with state boards of nursing on an annual basis to demonstrate that although it is a unique program, the outcomes are similar to traditional programs and graduate achievement is similar to traditional programs. Excelsior

College has also funded research by two independent organizations (Gwatkin, L., Hancock, M., Javitz, H., 2009; Darrah, M., Humbert, R., 2009) to examine graduate performance. This research has been shared with the NCSBN and boards of nursing in all 50 states and the District of Columbia.

Another lesson learned following the state board challenges relates to perception and messaging. Discussions with individual board members in Georgia and Virginia post-resolution revealed that many board members and deans of in-state programs perceived the college's activities as seeking to adhere to a different set of standards than required of in-state schools. The College assumed the opposition expressed by in-state schools resulted from a perceived threat to their enrollments. As a result, much of the communication with in-state programs was targeted toward explaining the difference in student populations and addressing the in-state schools' concern about enrollments. Perhaps, if the college had reinforced that we were not seeking in-state approval or registration, just licensure of our graduates based on our approval in New York; the process and resulting strained relationships with in-state schools would have been different. The College also learned that our alliance with the Georgia Nurses Association (GNA) did not assist us on our communication with the board of nursing or Representative Cooper. We learned after-the-fact that there were additional tensions between the board of nursing and the GNA that detracted from the college's efforts to seek a resolution to the problem. A lesson learned here is to seek advice from an independent agency with the ability to distinguish philosophical differences and political differences.

Probably the most important lesson learned from the state board challenges is that an out-of-state institution filing a lawsuit against a government agency can be damaging. The lawsuit against the California board of nursing occurred more than 10 years ago but the court's findings are still prominently posted on the board website. When representatives of the college visit with members of the board of nursing, professional nursing organizations, representatives of governmental agencies and legislative staffers, they are still greeted with, "you are the college that sued us." The lesson to be learned here is that even though individuals within the various stakeholder groups sympathized with the college position, they took offense at the action of filing suit against their "home" governmental agency. Even though the administration at the college and the board of nursing have all changed, the relationship between the board and the college remains contentious. It is anticipated that the long-term effects of this failed lawsuit will most likely endure for decades. This has been a very difficult lesson for the college and most importantly our graduates who wish to work as RNs in California. The process for achieving a legislative resolution is very lengthy, and may require many attempts during many legislative sessions, but the end result—regardless of outcome—will most likely be better than bringing suit against a governmental agency.

About the Contributors

Robin Berenson, Ph.D., has over 15 years of experience in online learning in higher education with particular emphasis in curriculum/ course development, accreditation, faculty mentoring, building virtual communities, competency-based education (CBE), and student success and retention. She is the former associate dean for business at Excelsior College, and has served as a dean, program chair, professor, instructional designer, and adjunct instructor for various online and traditional institutions.

Prior to her higher education experience, Dr. Berenson held executive leadership positions in health care and human resources. Her research explored emotional intelligence as a predictor of success in online learning, and she has presented and published on topics including competency-based education (CBE), faculty mentoring, student success, leadership, and emotional intelligence for women.

Dr. Berenson holds an EdD in Organizational Leadership from Argosy University of Sarasota, a MS in human resource development and management from Towson University, a BA in psychology from University of North Carolina at Charlotte, and is a certified job and career transition coach (JCTC).

Scott V. Dolan, Ph.D., is the executive director of accreditation, assessment, and strategy for the School of Business and Technology at Excelsior College, where he is responsible for the development and management of the outcome assessment process in all the degree programs in the School of Business and Technology, including programs with specialized accreditation from IACBE and ABET. Additionally, Dr. Dolan oversees the continuous improvement efforts of the school and leads the development, implementation, and evaluation of the School's strategic initiatives. Prior to his current appointment, Dr. Dolan worked for a private, nonprofit program evaluation firm in Albany, New York, conducting program evaluations of P-20 education programs. Dr. Dolan received his doctoral degree in sociology from the University at Albany-State University of New York.

John Ebersole, Ed.D., has been president of Excelsior College since January of 2006. Prior to assuming his current position, he served as a Senior Fellow at Harvard 's Kennedy School of Government, while also concluding a six-year assignment as Associate Provost at Boston University. Other work in higher education has included administrative and faculty positions at Colorado State University, the University of California, Berkeley, and John F. Kennedy University. Prior to commencing a career in higher education, Dr. Ebersole completed a series of assignments in the U.S. Coast Guard, where he held two afloat commands, including one in Vietnam. During his 21 years in uniform, Ebersole held a number of posts in training and professional development, including command of the Pacific Area Training Team.

Dr. Ebersole's education has included attendance at twelve different institutions, ranging from Long Beach City College to Oxford. He holds master's degrees in both public and business administration, is a distinguished graduate of the U.S. Naval War College, and has an earned doctorate in law and policy from Northeastern University. He also holds an Education Specialist designation from the George Washington University.

Active in adult and online learning, Ebersole has been inducted into the halls of fame of both the U.S. Distance Education Association and the International Association of Continuing Education. He is also the recipient of a Distinguished Public Service Award from the Secretary of the Army (for efforts in support of education for U.S. Army personnel). Ebersole's professional service has included serving as president of the University Professional and Continuing Education Association; chair of the Commission on Lifelong Learning, American Council on Education; and director and chair of the Academic Affairs Committee, New England College of Finance. Currently he serves as chair of Lighthouse Academies Charter School network and is a member of the board of directors for both the New York Commission on Independent Colleges and Universities and the Presidents Forum.

An advocate for post traditional adult learners and online education, his comments are often found in the online editions of Forbes and the Huffington Post. His book *Courageous Learning* (Hudson Whitman; 2013) was written with Bill Patrick. It has since been made into a television documentary under the same title.

Tina Goodyear is the executive director of the Center for the Assessment of Post-Traditional Instruction, Training, and Learning at Excelsior College in Albany, NY, chief operating officer for the Presidents' Forum, and the former director of the USNY Regents Research Fund National College Credit Recommendation Service. Tina is working on her dissertation for an EdD in leadership and management at Capella University; she holds an MS in education from the State University of New York at Albany and a BA in English from the University of Connecticut, Storrs. Her expertise and areas of interest include nontraditional education, prior learning assessment, and translating workplace training and credentialing programs into college credit. She has served on the advisory council for CAEL's LearningCounts.org; as an expert panel for SUNY Empire State College's Global Qualifications Learning Framework project; as a member of the New York State Regents' task force on competency-based education, and as a member of the Council on Higher Education Accreditation and Presidents' Forum Commission on Quality Assurance and Alternative Higher Education. She is currently working on a collaborative grant-funded project exploring quality assurance for nontraditional providers in the higher education sector.

Mika Hoffman, Ph.D., is the executive director of Test Development Services at Excelsior College. She has worked at the Department of Defense as the Dean of the Test Development Division at the Defense Language Institute Foreign Language Center in Monterey, California, where she managed the high-stakes Defense Language Proficiency Testing program. She earned a BA with High Honors from Swarthmore College, an MA with Distinction in the Teaching of Foreign Languages (French) from the Monterey Institute of International Studies, and a Ph. D. in Linguistics from the Massachusetts Institute of Technology.

Patrick Jones, Ph.D., is vice provost at Excelsior College. He received his PhD in measurement, evaluation and applied statistics from Columbia University in 1987. He has presented and published primarily in the areas of outcomes assessment, accreditation policies and procedures, computer-based testing, equating, scaling and standard-setting procedures. He has served as a reviewer for and contributor to the annual meeting of the American Educational Research Association, the National Council on Measurement in Education, the American Psychological Association, and the Association of Test Publishers. Dr. Jones has over 40 publications and presentations in the areas of educational measurement and cognitive psychology. He currently volunteers as a consulting psychometrician for the accreditation board for Specialty Nursing Certification, and formerly served as a public representative on the board of directors of the American Board of Perianesthesia Nursing Certification, Inc. and a commissioner on the ANSI Personnel Certification Accreditation Committee. Dr. Jones joined Excelsior College in April 2002 after 20 years of service at the Professional Examination Service (PES) in New York, NY. From 1997 to 2002, he was executive vice president at PES. Prior to assuming the vice provost position in 2011, Patrick served as the dean of the Assessment Unit at Excelsior along with interim positions as dean of the School of Business and Technology, co-dean of the School of Liberal Arts, and director of the Institutional Research and Outcomes Assessment units.

Karl G. Lawrence, Ph.D., FRM, CFP®, is dean of the School of Business and Technology at Excelsior College. He received his doctoral degree in finance from Florida State University. He also earned an MBA with a concentration in international business from Florida International University. He is currently the chair of the Business and Economics Department at Fort Valley State University. Prior to his current appointment, Dr. Lawrence served an assistant professor at Florida A&M University, where he coordinated the university's very successful Wall Street initiative. Dr. Lawrence is credited with developing the Florida State Board of Administration risk management plan and has been involved with risk management for over 15 years.

Dr. Lawrence is also the founder and former executive director of American Financial Institute, a not-for-profit organization that offers professional licensure/certification courses, financial literacy workshops, and vocational rehabilitation services. He is also the founder and former president of Lawrence Construction Management, a firm that specializes in the development and construction of middle-market single-family homes. Dr. Lawrence's knowledge within the field of finance spans a wide spectrum. He is a certified financial planner and financial risk manager, as well as a licensed real estate and general appraisal instructor and a mortgage broker instructor. He also serves as an economic expert witness in civil liability cases.

Mary Lee Pollard, Ph.D., is the dean of the School of Nursing at Excelsior College. In this role, she assures that a high-quality, affordable, and accessible education is provided annually to approximately 21,000 undergraduate and graduate nursing students nationwide. Under her direction, Excelsior's School of Nursing graduates an average of 1,900 students per year, advancing healthcare throughout the United States. Dr. Pollard is an expert in competency-based nursing education. In recognition of her skillful program management, she has been invited to serve as a panelist in forums hosted by the Center for American Progress and the Council on Adult and Experiential Learning, and has also provided presentations on the competency-based education at national conferences.

Advancing a diverse population of nurses along a career ladder is a priority for Dr. Pollard. She is a member of the New York State Associate Degree Council of Nurse Educators, the New York State Council of Deans of Baccalaureate and Higher Programs, the National Organization for Associate Degree Nursing, the National League for Nursing, and the National Association of Hispanic Nurses; and she serves on the board of the Tau Kappa chapter of Sigma Theta Tau. She is a past board member of the New York State Nurses Association District 9 and the New York State Associate Degree Council of Nurse Educators, and she also served on the steering committee for the Helene Fuld Health Trust initiative for the New York State Coalition for Nursing Educational Mobility to develop a statewide LPN to RN articulation model.

A strong believer in utilizing research to inform both nursing education and practice, she is a board member of the Capital District Nursing Research Alliance. She recently served as the primary investigator for a study titled *Assessment of Quality and Safety Education in Nursing: A New York State Perspective.* Her areas of expertise are nontraditional nursing student attrition, competency assessment, and adult education.

ABOUT HUDSON WHITMAN

Hudson Whitman is a small press affiliated with Excelsior College, which has its administrative offices in Albany, New York.

Our tagline is "Books That Make a Difference" and we strive to publish high-quality nonfiction books and multimedia projects in areas that complement Excelsior's interest in health, military, and alternative higher education.

If you would like to submit a manuscript or proposal, please feel free to review the guidelines on our website, www.hudsonwhitman.com. We will respond within 6–8 weeks.

OTHER TITLES BY HUDSON WHITMAN

See Me for Who I Am: Student Veterans' Stories of War and Coming Home
Edited by David Chrisinger

Courageous Learning: Finding a New Path through Higher Education
John Ebersole

Retire the Colors: Veterans & Civilians on Iraq & Afghanistan
Edited by Dario DiBattista

The Call of Nursing: Stories from the Front Lines of Health Care
William Patrick

Shot: Staying Alive with Diabetes
Amy Ryan

The Sanctuary of Illness: A Memoir of Heart Disease
Thomas Larson

N21: Nursing in the 21st Century
An open access, multimedia, mobile journal, available on our website.